St. Helena Library

P9-BIC-597

ST. HELENA PUBLIC LIBRARY
1492 LIBRARY LANE
ST. HELENA, CA 94574-1143
(707) 963-5244

THE STATES OF
NORTHERN MEXICO

DEIRDRE DAY-MACLEOD

108°W   106°W   104°W   102°W

32°N

Ciudad Juárez

UNITED STATES

100°W   98°W

30°N

N

W   E

S

28°N

CHIHUAHUA

Chihuahua

COAHUILA

Nuevo
Laredo

26°N

MEXICO

NUEVO
LEÓN

Reynosa
Matamoros

Tarreón

Saltillo

Monterrey

24°N

DURANGO

Durango

ZACATECAS

Ciudad
Victoria

Gulf of Mexico

PACIFIC
OCEAN

TAMAULIPAS

Zacatecas

22°N

SAN LUIS
POTOSÍ

0   100   200 Miles

San Luis Potosí

0   100   200 Kilometers
Albers Conic Equal-Area Projection

2/04

J 97~

OUR SOUTHERN NEIGHBOR
MEXICO

THE STATES OF NORTHERN MEXICO

DIERDRE DAY-MACLEOD

Mason Crest Publishers
Philadelphia

Mason Crest Publishers
370 Reed Road
Broomall PA 19008
www.masoncrest.com

Copyright © 2003 by Mason Crest Publishers. All rights reserved.

First printing

1 3 5 7 9 8 6 4 2

Library of Congress Cataloging-in-Publication Data on file at the Library of Congress

ISBN 1-59084-086-0

TABLE OF CONTENTS

OUR SOUTHERN NEIGHBOR MEXICO

Roger E. Hernández
Senior Consulting Editor

INTRODUCTION

exico is a country in the midst of great change. And what happens in Mexico will have an important impact on the United States, its neighbor to the north.

These changes are being put in place by President Vicente Fox, who was elected in 2000. For the previous 71 years, power had been held by presidents from one single party, known in Spanish as *Partido Revolucionario Institucional* (Institutional Revolutionary Party, or PRI). Some of those presidents have been accused of corruption. President Fox, from a different party called *Partido de Acción Nacional* (National Action Party, or PAN), says he wants to eliminate that corruption. He also wants to have a friendlier relationship with the United States, and for American businesses to increase trade with Mexico. That will create more jobs, he says, and decrease poverty—which in turn will mean fewer Mexicans will find themselves forced to emigrate in search of a better life.

But it would be wrong to think of Mexico as nothing more than a poor country. Mexico has given the world some of its greatest artists and writers. Carlos Fuentes is considered one of the greatest living novelists, and poet-essayist Octavio Paz was awarded the Nobel Prize for Literature in 1990, the most prestigious honor a writer can win. Painters such as Diego Rivera and José Clemente Orozco specialized in murals, huge paintings done on walls that tell of the history of the nation. Another famous Mexican painter, Rufino Tamayo, blended the "cubist" style of modern European painters like Picasso with native folk themes.

Tamayo's paintings in many ways symbolize what Mexico is: A blend of the culture of Europe (more specifically, its Spanish version) and the indigenous cultures that predated the arrival of Columbus.

Those cultures were thriving even 3,000 years ago, when the Olmec people built imposing monuments that survive to this day in what are now the states of Tabasco and Veracruz. Later and further to the south in the Yucatán Peninsula, the Maya civilization flourished. They constructed cities in the midst of the jungle, complete with huge temples, courts in which ball games were played, and highly accurate calendars intricately carved in stone pillars. For some mysterious reason, the Mayans abandoned most of these great centers 1,100 years ago.

The Toltecs, in central Mexico, were the next major civilization. They were followed by the Aztecs. It was the Aztecs who built the city of Tenochitlán in the middle of a lake in what is now Mexico City, with long causeways connecting it to the mainland. By the early 1500s it was one of the largest cities anywhere, with perhaps 200,000 inhabitants.

Then the Spanish came. In 1519, twenty-seven years after Columbus arrived in the Americas, Hernán Cortés landed in Yucatán with just 600 soldiers plus a few cannons and horses. They marched inland, gaining allies as they went along among indigenous peoples who resented being ruled by the Aztecs. Within two years Cortés and the Spaniards ruled Mexico. They had conquered the Aztec Empire and devastated their great capital.

It was in that destruction that modern Mexico was born. The influence of the Aztecs and other indigenous people did not disappear even though untold numbers were killed. But neither can Mexico be recognized today without the Spanish influence.

Spain ruled for three centuries. Then in 1810 Mexicans began a struggle for independence from colonial Spain, much like the United States had fought for its own independence from Great Britain. In 1821 Mexico finally became an independent nation.

The newly born republic faced many difficulties. There was much poverty, especially among descendants of indigenous peoples; most of the wealth and political power was in the hands of a small elite of Spanish ancestry. To make things worse, Mexico lost almost half of its territory to the United States in a war that lasted from 1846 to 1848. Many still resent the loss of territory, which accounts for lingering anti-American sentiments among some Mexicans. The country was later occupied by France, but under national hero Benito Juárez Mexico regained its independence in 1867.

The next turning point in Mexican history came in 1911, when a revolution meant to help the millions of Mexicans stuck in poverty began against dictator Porfirio Díaz. There was violence and fighting until 1929, when Plutarco Elías Calles founded what was to become the *Partido Revolucionario Institucional*. It brought stability as well as economic progress. Yet millions of Mexicans remained in poverty, and as time went on PRI rulers became increasingly corrupt.

It was the desire of the people of Mexico to trust someone other than the candidate of PRI that resulted in the election of Fox. And so this nation of more than 100 million, with its ancient heritage, its diverse mestizo culture, its grinding poverty, and its glorious arts, stands on the brink of a new era. Modern Mexico is seeking a place as the leader of all Latin America, an ally of the United States, and an important voice in global politics. For that to happen, Mexico must narrow the gap between the rich and poor and bring more people in the middle class. It will be interesting to watch as Fox and the Mexican people work to bring their country into the first rank of nations.

An old church is tucked into a canyon in the Sierra Madre Mountains of Chihuahua. Many of Mexico's colonial buildings remain standing throughout the country.

THE LAND

I magine Mexico as a giant letter "vee" with its the top opening toward the United States. Two rugged mountain ranges form the edges of the vee—the "Mother" mountains: the Sierra Madre Oriental and the Sierra Madre Occidental. In the north, they are wide apart, separated by the *Meseta Central* (the Central **Plateau**). The northern states of Mexico lie within the top of this vee. This region is composed of seven states: Chihuahua, Coahuila, Durango, Nuevo León, San Luis Potosí, Tamaulipas, and Zacetecas.

When you look at a map of Mexico it is difficult to tell which areas are *tierra caliente, tierra templada,* or *tierra fria*—the hot-, medium-, and cold-weather areas. This is because the climate in Mexico is determined not by whether the land is in the north or the south as much as by elevation—the higher up in the mountains, the cooler the region. Much of this area falls into the medium-weather or temperate zone. The state of Tamaulipas, which lies along the Gulf Coast, however, is *tierra caliente,* as is the northernmost part of the land that slopes down toward the Río Grande.

The northern edge of this area lies along the Río Grande, the 2,000-mile border river shared with the United States. The Río Grande, called the Río Bravo by the Mexicans, is a shallow winding river that empties into the Gulf of Mexico. It brings together rivers from all along the eastern side of Mexico.

The Chihuahua Desert lies just south of the Río Grande. In the native language, Chihuahua means "dry, sandy land," and the Chihuahua is the largest desert in North America. This desert covers about 175,000 square miles and is bigger than the entire state of California. It is called a "rain shadow desert," because the two mountain ranges on either side of it stop the moist air from the Gulf of Mexico and the Pacific Ocean from reaching the middle area. Unlike many deserts, the Chihuahua is not flat. There are many small mountain ranges running through it, and within the cracks between mountains are river basins. The differences in altitude mean that the Chihuahua is home to more kinds of wildlife than most other deserts.

The Indians who once inhabited this area could not farm but lived by hunting and gathering, sometimes eating the cactus or even iguanas and insects. There are 500 different kinds of cactus in Mexico, and Indians once used some of them for food and drink. The dry land cannot support much life unless it is *irrigated*.

Deep canyons cut through this rough scenery. The flat area, called "Meseta Central"—the central plateau—is cradled between the two jagged mountain ranges. The land sloping toward the Río Grande has become a region of large cities with sky scrapers and factories. It is also a land where there are still Indians living in caves. Orchards and

This vibrantly striped kingsnake can be found in the mountains of Durango. The range of climates of Mexico create comfortable habitats for a unique variety of animals, reptiles, and birds.

croplands flourish in fertile valleys reclaimed by irrigation.

The area known as Copper Canyon is twice the size of the Grand Canyon in Arizona. Copper Canyon is not a single canyon but the union of several deep, spectacular canyons. It is cut by the Urique River and has deep, wide gorges so remote that parts of it have never been explored on foot. This region is also known as the Sierra Tarahumara, after the Indians who live there. No copper is found here; the canyon is named for the color of its walls.

The Sierra Madre Occidental forms the western rim of the Plateau of Mexico, and it runs from Chihuahua down through Durango and then into Zacatecas, the Mexican states that lie to the south. For hundreds of years, this mountain range blocked transportation between the plateau and the west coast, forming a natural barrier. Paved roads and a railroad were not built across it until the 1900s.

The Chihuahua Desert stretches across several Mexican states, as well as across the border and into the United States. This fishhook barrel cactus thrives in Nuevo León.

This range includes some of Mexico's most rugged land. Short, steep streams flowing to the Pacific Ocean have cut canyons more than a mile (1.6 kilometers) deep through the mountains.

Higher in the mountains, the weather gets colder. Here bear and sheep live. In the winter the forests at the tops of the mountains may be covered in snow, while the valleys beneath are still tropically warm. These western mountains climb to the height of 9,200 feet. The Rarahumura Indians *migrate* from the caves where they live in the summer, down to the warmer areas when frigid winter winds arrive. The state of Durango is also famous for its huge desert scorpions.

The Sierra Madre Oriental, the plateau's eastern rim, runs through the states of Coahuila and Nuevo León. These mountains are actually a series of ranges. In many places, between the ranges, highways and railroads climb up to the plateau from the east coast. Though

These Tarahumara Indian girls are wearing traditional dresses. The Tarahumara are descended from natives of Mexico. Most live in the Sierra Madre Mountains apart from Mexico's *mestizo* civilization.

the Sierra Madre Oriental is not a region of abundance agriculturally, this area is rich in metals such as silver, gold, lead, iron, and zinc.

In Tamaulipas, beside the Gulf of Mexico, the land is flat and low with marshes and lagoons, alligators and crocodiles. This is *tierra caliente* or hot land. Tamaulipas borders the United States on the north, Veracruz and San Luis Potosí to the south, Veracruz and the Gulf of Mexico to the east. In the native people's language, the name may mean "High Mountains," "Tribe of Olives," or "Place of Much Prayer." In the north, Tamaulipas is fairly dry and warm with only a little rain. In the south and southeast it is warmer and wetter. In the mountains, the climate ranges from warm to temperate according to altitude.

There are places in Tamaulipas so remote that the people who live there don't use money. Many of these live in a protected region called

Intricate and elaborate sculpture surrounds the altarpiece in a side chapel of the Templo de Carmen in San Luis Potosí. The Roman Catholic religion dominates Mexico, with about 90 percent of the population members of the church.

the "El Cielo" biosphere reserve. This is an area where all the wildlife and plants are protected from harm.

The Huasteca is the region of the Sierra Madre Oriental that covers the south of Tamaulipas as well as the northern region of San Luis Potosí (and Veracruz). It rains there between 60 and 150 inches annually. Much of the Huasteca is covered with tropical cloud forests. Here you can find spectacular waterfalls, cenotes (sinkholes), and lush canyons that are an amazing contrast to the to the high dry deserts just a few hours away.

CHIHUAHUA

Location: Sonora lies to the west; Coahuila to the east; the United States to the north; and Durango to the south.

Capital: Chihuahua

Total area: 96,364 square miles (247,087 sq km)

Climate: Mostly dry and warm; colder at higher elevations

Terrain: Desert, canyons, some forests at higher elevations

Elevation: High 10,725 feet (3,250 meters) Low 4,921 feet (1,500 meters)

Natural hazards: Drought, earthquakes

COAHUILA

Location: The United States lies to the north; Nuevo León to the east; San Luis Potosí and Zacatecas to the south; and Durango and Chihuahua to the northeast.

Capital: Saltillo

Total area: 58,493 square miles (149,982 sq km)

Climate: Mild, dry

Terrain: Deserts and mountains

Elevation: High 12,172 feet (3,700 meters) Low 2,625 feet (800 meters)

Natural hazards: Earthquakes

DURANGO

Location: Chihuahua and Coahuila lie to the north; Zacatecas to the east; Nayarit to the south; and Sinaloa to the west.

Capital: Durango

Total area: 46,663 square miles (119,648 sq km)

Climate: Moderate with four seasons

Terrain: Mountainous

Elevation: High 10,956 feet (3,320 meters) Low

Natural hazards: Earthquakes

18

NUEVO LEÓN

Location: Surrounded by Coahuila to the west and north; Tamaulipas to the east; San Luis Potosí and Zacatecas to the south.

Capital: Guadalupe

Total area:
25,176 square miles
(64,555 sq km)

Climate: Hot, humid

Terrain: Mountainous

Elevation: High 12,139 feet (3,700 meters) Low 2,953 feet
(900 meters)

Natural hazards:
Earthquakes, mud slides

SAN LUIS POTOSÍ

Location: Coahuila lies to the south, Nuevo León and Tamaulipas to the northeast; Veracruz to the east; Guanajuato, Querétaro, and Hidalgo to the south; and Zacatecas to the west.

Capital: San Luis Potosí

Total area:
24,511 square miles
(62,848 sq km)

Climate: Tropical to cool and arid, depending on altitude.

Terrain: Mountainous

Elevation: High 9,843 feet (3,000 meters) Low 223 feet
(68 meters)

Natural hazards:
Earthquakes

TAMUALIPAS

Location: The United States lies to the north; Veracruz and San Luis Potosí are to the south; the Gulf of Mexico is to the east; and Nuevo León is to the west.

Capital: Ciudad Victoria

Total area: 31,133 square miles (79,829 sq km)

Climate: The north-central part is semi-dry and semi-warm, with scarce rain. The south and southeast parts are warm, with summer rains.

Terrain: Mountainous away from the coast

Elevation: High 9,843 feet (3,000 meters) Low Sea level

Natural hazards: Hurricanes

ZACATECAS

Location: Durango lies to the northwest; Coahuila to the northeast; San Luis Potosí to the east; and Jalisco and Aguascalientes to the south.

Capital: Zacatecas

Total area: 58,654 square miles (150,395 sq km)

Climate: Four types of climate, depending on altitude: semi-warm, dry, mild, and cold.

Terrain: Mountainous

levation: High 10,499 feet (3,200 meters) Low 6,594 feet (2,010 meters)

Natural hazards: Earthquakes, volcanoes

A statue of a horse and rider in the Gran Plaza, Monterrey. The northern states of Mexico have played an important part in Mexico's history.

THE HISTORY

The stories that have come to us about the history of the northern parts of Mexico are as beautiful and as brutal as the land itself. Long ago, tribes called Chichimecas lived in these desert regions. They could not grow food in land that had no water, nor could they raise livestock. They wandered from place to place, wintering in the warmer parts and spending their summers up higher in the mountains. They would eat whatever they could find—snakes, reptiles, cactus, even insects. In the mountains, they could catch rabbits or gather wild foods.

These Chichimecas—the name given to all of the northern nomads regardless of their tribe—came down from northern Mexico to settle in the central region—the meseta—where the land was fertile and more forgiving. The word "Chichimeca" meant "lineage of the dog," but it was not meant as an insult. Rather, many Aztec dynasties were proud to claim this heritage. But while the Aztecs swept across central Mexico, conquering the other tribes, the people who remained in the north continued to live as they had. Some, such as the Rarahumurai, live in this fashion even today.

When the Spanish arrived, conquering the northern part of Mexico took them much longer than they had needed to control the central region of Mexico. For generations, roving tribes would come down from the mountains, attack the Spanish, and then retreat. The Spanish settlers who were brave enough to venture into northern Mexico were not *conquistadors* seeking treasure and fame. Instead, these were people who planned to stay—miners and ranchers and Catholic priests.

Between A.D. 1000 and 1200, the ancient city of Paquimé thrived in the area that today is the state of Chihuahua. It was the most important trading and farming center in northern Mexico. The people who lived there kept parrots and turkeys in pens; they built *aqueducts* and *cisterns* to supply their city with fresh water. By the time the Spanish came to Mexico, however, the people of Paquimé had disappeared, and the Aztecs had burned their abandoned buildings. Archeologists did not discover the long-ago city until the 1970s.

When the Spanish came to this land, they brought with them horses, cattle, and sheep—and the desert became ranchland that at one time stretched beyond the Río Grande into what is now the United States. The new animals from Europe altered the landscape. It became rangeland, where vast *haciendas* stretched for miles and miles. In Chihuahua, *vaqueros* originated the riding and roping skills we now associate with American cowboys.

The land was secluded and wild, separated from civilization by the desert's sandstorms. During the Mexican Revolution, this seclusion appealed to Pancho Villa, the rebel leader. He established his headquarters in Chihuahua; his band of cowboys and bandits streamed out of the

This mural depicts aspects of the life of ancient Aztecs. Murals are popular throughout Mexico, both inside and outside buildings.

desert to attack the unjust government of Porfirio Díaz—and then they retreated back to the safety of the desert.

COAHUILA

The state of Coahuila is proud of the part it played in Mexican history. Two great leaders of the nation's fight for freedom and equal rights were born in Saltillo, the state's capital city. The first of these, Francisco Madero, was the first political leader to seize power from Porfirio Díaz, whose harsh rule controlled Mexico for more than 30 years. Madero, a wealthy landowner, challenged Díaz in the elections, and as a result Madero was imprisoned. After his release, Madero fled to the United States, where he called for revolution in Mexico. Under his leadership, the

One of the most influential revolutionaries of his time, Francisco "Pancho" Villa was considered a champion of the Mexican Revolution in the early 20th century.

Mexican Revolution was launched, and Díaz was overthrown.

The second revolutionary leader to come from Coahuila was Venustiano Carranza. He was a military general who is called the

"Father of the Mexican Constitution." He became the governor of his state, and then went on to become the nation's president.

DURANGO

When the Spanish began to settle northern Mexico, their coming nearly destroyed the native people who already lived there. The Spanish turned the Indians into slaves; many of the native people died because they had no *immunities* to the diseases the Spanish brought with them; and the Spanish missionaries tried to take away the Indians' religion and replace it with Christianity.

But some of the native people fought back. In Durango, between 1616 and 1620, the Tepehuán people fought for their freedom and their rights. The rebellion was led by a man named Quautlatas, who had been flogged by the *Jesuit* missionaries for expressing his doubts about Christianity. Quautlatas encouraged his people to reject Christianity, to recover their faith in their old beliefs, and to drive the

Francisco Indalecio Madeno was a Mexican revolutionary and politician. He opposed President Díaz and took over the presidency for two years, until his reign was overthown.

Spanish invaders out of their land. He traveled from settlement to settlement, fanning the fires of rebellion. He told his listeners that if they were killed in battle against the Spanish, they would be brought back to life seven days after their final victory.

The rebels burned churches and killed more than 400 Spanish settlers and missionaries. The Spanish responded by sending their troops to kill and defeat the Tepehuánes. More than a thousand of the native people were killed, and hundreds more were sold into slavery.

ZACATECAS

Durango was not the only region to experience Indian rebellion. In 1541, Indians in the area that is now Zacatecas burned down the churches and killed the owners of the haciendas. The Spanish swiftly and brutally squashed the uprising, forcing the Indians to flee into the highlands of Zacetecas, a land of steep hills and poisonous scorpions.

After this war, known as the Mixton War, the Spanish felt that they must overpower all the Indians. From Zacetecas, the Spanish moved to conquer the whole area of north-central Mexico. As mines flourished and farms were established, more and more Indians were either made into slaves or forced farther north to less desirable land.

NUEVO LEÓN

When the Spanish conquered this region they gave it the name of Nuevo Reino de León in honor of Reino of León, an area in Spain. In September 20, 1596, Don Diego de Montemayor, a Spanish conquistador, settled a city here with 12 families. At that time, the city was called Villa of San Luis

Rey of France, but Don Diego later changed the name to Ciudad Metropolitana de Nuestra Señora de Monterrey. Four hundred years later, Monterrey is a modern and industrial city, the third largest in Mexico.

SAN LUIS POTOSÍ

This region was first settled in 1583 as a Franciscan mission, but the community forgot its preoccupation with religion when someone discovered silver in the mountains. Because of the royal fortune beneath the land, it was given a new, royal name in 1592—San Luis, after King Louis IX of France. Potosí was the name of a rich Bolivian mining town, and this was tacked on as well, in hopes that this region would prove to be as prosperous as the Bolivian town.

By the 19th century, however, San Luis Potosí had become an out-of-the-way refuge for political liberals who were seeking to escape government persecution. After Napoleon's troops captured Mexico City in 1863, President Juárez brought the remains of his government to San Luis—but then he moved still further north, into Chihuahua.

At the time of the Mexican Revolution, San Luis was still a haven for liberal opposition to the government. Francisco Madero fled here after Díaz arrested him for challenging his presidency. Madero moved on across the border to San Antonio, Texas, but when he drafted his famous plan for a new government, he called it the *Plan de San Luis Potosí*. Madero managed to win his fight against Díaz, but he did not hold the presidency long. By 1913 he had been assassinated, and the revolution splintered in many warring factions.

Vicente Fox was elected president of Mexico in 2000. He was the first president of the country from a political party other than the Party of the Institutionalized Revolution (PRI), which had held power for seven decades.

TAMAULIPAS

During the 1830s, the people of Tamaulipas opposed the central government's rule. They felt that the Mexican government was only plunging them into deeper and deeper economic trouble. They supported a **petition** that asked that the president get rid of the existing **cabinet**, and create an entirely new government.

At the time, Tamaulipas, Coahuila, Nuevo León, and Texas were a single military jurisdiction. Texas eventually achieved its independence from the Mexican government, but Tamaulipas, along with Coahuila and Nuevo León, remained under the Mexican government's repressive control until the Revolution of 1910 brought the entire nation greater freedom.

ZACATECAS

In the mid-16th century, a native Cascane from this region gave a silver trinket to one of the early Spanish colonists. The silver, the Cascane said, had come from the mountains of this land. The small gift sparked the mining rush that continued for the next two centuries. During these years more than a billion dollars worth of silver and other precious metals were stripped from the hills of Zacatecas.

By the 20th century, the mines were running dry, but Zacatecas still had an important part to play in Mexican history. The rebel leader Pancho Villa fought an important battle here during the Mexican Revolution, defeating the government's troops.

Northern Mexico may be a harsh and isolated land—but Mexico would not be the nation it is today without the part the northern states played in their country's history. After centuries of internal strife, today Mexico looks toward the future under the new leadership of Vicente Fox. Fox was elected president in 2000, and he has vowed to do all he can to heal the wounds of his country's troubled past.

A farmer stands among the dry stalks of corn in his field. In recent years, Mexico has been plagued by repeated droughts, making farming a particularly difficult way to make a living.

THE ECONOMY

Mexico has a long history of serious economic problems. The gap between the rich and the poor has been wide and deep, and the government has often done very little to solve the problems of a desperately poor population. Instead, year after year, the nation's economy grew weaker and weaker, while the government made a series of foolish decisions.

Today, however, Mexico is struggling to heal some of the many problems that have scarred its economy. The North American Free Trade Agreement (NAFTA) is one of the key factors in the economic growth of Mexico. This is especially true of the northern states that are so close to the U.S.–Mexican border.

NAFTA was negotiated between the United States, Mexico, and Canada in 1991, it was completed in 1993, and it became active on January 1, 1994. One goal of NAFTA is to remove trade restrictions between the countries over a 15-year time period. Import duties are abolished between participating countries. This means a country does not have to pay a tax to sell products from one country to another. The agreement brings Mexico into one of the largest trade zones in the world. NAFTA removes barriers and therefore speeds up the process of buying and selling. It provides more opportunities for investment and encourages cooperation between nations.

NAFTA is not the answer to all of the economic growth in Mexico, however. In some instances, in fact, it has created problems. In 1995, under President Zedillo, there was a financial crisis from an imbalance in trade. More was going out of the country than was coming in. *Interest rates* went up and people were having a hard time paying for necessary items. By 1999, however, Mexico's economic situation had begun to improve.

Maquiladoras have created much of the growth. The *maquiladoras* are assembly plants where the pieces of a product are **imported** into Mexico without any tax. The product is assembled in Mexico. It is then **exported** from Mexico, again without paying a tax. U.S. businesses are attracted to Mexican *maquiladoras* because they do not have to obey American safety regulations or pay their workers as much as they would have to in the United States; this means the factory owners can make their products more cheaply and sell them at a greater profit. Around the world, many people are concerned about the poor working conditions in Mexican *maquiladoras*.

However, despite the poor working conditions, and even though most of these plants or factories are owned by foreigners, they still boost the economy by providing jobs. This creates the need for more technology. More electricity, running water, housing, roads, and transportation are needed to support all of the people who are working in the *maquiladoras*.

A train runs along the Copper Canyon in the Sierra Madre Mountains. Mexico's tumultuous history and limited finances have brought about few improvements in its infrastructure and technology.

Nuevo León is is one of Mexico's leading industrial areas. It is easy to pass across a new international bridge to the United States, and there are numerous factories that produce iron and steel, glass, textiles, and petrochemicals. Monterrey is the financial center; the city's 123 maquiladoras employ 20,560 people. Forty percent of the jobs in this state involve manufacturing. In fact, Nuevo León is one of the few places in Mexico where unemployment is not a problem. The government is working to train people to work in the factories because of a shortage of skilled labor.

However, due to the extreme heat and dryness, not much grows in Nuevo León. Cattle raising is the primary agricultural activity.

Silver purses hang for sale at a tourist market. Mexico's folk art is appreciated both inside and outside its borders. Tourism and the souvenir business are thriving.

Good railroads and highways in San Luis Potosí make transporting goods easy. Agriculture and cattle also play an important role in San Luis Potosí's economy. Most of the industry concerns automobiles, mining, food processing, mechanics, textiles, and beverage production. Although San Luis Potosí began as a mining settlement, today most of its economy is built around exporting goods.

The economy of Zacetecas depends mainly on agriculture, livestock, and mining. Main products include guavas, grapes, peaches, and apples. Cattle and sheep graze on more than half the land. Mining of silver, tin, lead, copper, and gold continues. Most of Mexico's silver comes from Zacetecas.

A young Tarahumara boy stands in a field. Farming is an essential part of Mexico's economy, and it provides the necessities for the family who must work the land.

Durango's economic strength is mining and forestry. More than a third of Mexico's timber comes from this state. Wood-related industries make paper, plywood, cross ties, and other wooden items. Most of the industry is located in Ciudad Lerdo and in Gomez Palacio. One third of Durango's economy is based on the farming of crops and livestock.

In Tamaulipas, agriculture is important. Efficient irrigation allows farmers to grow sorghum, wheat, and corn. Fishing along the coast depends upon shrimp, crayfish, oyster, and crabs. Oil production and maquiladoras account for most of the industry. The port of Tampico is one of the most active in the area.

Hand-made bricks dry in the yard of a brick factory near Durango. Manufacturing and industry have become key to Mexico's financial future.

Coahuila gets most of its income from mining and industry. Excellent highways allow goods to be transported easily. Fluorite, lead, and tin mining are important to this state's economy. Foundries take the raw materials and make steel and iron. Irrigation allows for farming and livestock raising. The area of Laguna is one of Mexico's richest farming regions.

Chihuahua, Mexico's largest state, depends on mining and industry for 36 percent of its economy. Most of the manufacturing occurs in maquiladoras along the U.S. border, in the two large cities, Ciudad Juárez and Chihuahua City. Ciudad Juárez remains the major manufacturing area, with about 400 factories in the same town that was at one time a stopping place for cowboys from El Paso. At the beginning of the last century, Chihuahua's economy was more concerned with timber and livestock, but today companies such as Toshiba, JRC, and Honeywell have factories here. In addition, Chihuahua has a number of tourist attractions, including the Copper Canyon.

Although there is no copper in Copper Canyon, the Spanish did find gold and silver as well as turquoise and amethyst there. Today many of the precious metals are gone, but a few prospectors are still trying to make a living there.

The Indians farm along the rivers, primarily raising corn. Almost every family tends to one milpa or cornfield, and there are six types of corn commonly grown here. Other important crops are beans, squash, peaches, apples, and potatoes.

CHIHUAHUA

GDP in thousands of pesos:
183,624,001
Percent of GDP:
Manufacturing 11 percent
Commerce 52 percent
Service industries 37 percent
Per capita income in pesos: 19,817
Exports: Minerals, corn, wheat,
beans, and meat.
Natural resources: timber, livestock

DURANGO

GDP in thousands of pesos:
52,542,937
Percent of GDP:
Manufacturing 13 percent
Commerce 53 percent
Service industries 34 percent
Per capita income: 12,672
Exports: Fruits, dairy products,
textiles, beans, and cotton.
Natural resources: forestry, mining

COAHUILA

GDP in thousands of pesos:
133,950,269
Percent of GDP:
Manufacturing 11 percent
Commerce 53 percent
Service industries 36 percent
Per capita income in pesos: 19,265
Exports: Iron, cotton, grapes, and
livestock.
Natural resources: iron ore, lead,
silver, zinc, gold, and copper

NUEVO LEÓN

GDP in thousands of pesos:
286,969,565
Percent of GDP:
Manufacturing 12 percent
Commerce 51 percent
Service industries 37 percent
Per capita income in pesos: 24,665
Exports: Glass, glassware, prepared
food stuffings, iron, beverages, and
chemicals
Natural resources: lead, iron ore,
copper

SAN LUIS POTOSÍ

GDP in thousands of pesos:
70,675,085
Percent of GDP:
Manufacturing 12 percent
Commerce 53 percent
Service industries 35 percent
Per capita income in pesos: 10,310
Exports: Minerals, precious metals, chemicals & tropical fruits
Natural resources: agriculture, silver, gold, lead

TAMAULIPAS

GDP in thousands of pesos:
41,998,268
Percent of GDP:
Manufacturing 9 percent
Commerce 51 percent
Service industries 40 percent
Per capita income in pesos: 15,288
Exports: Petrochemicals, fish, and crustaceans.
Natural resources: gold, copper, silver, lead, oil, fish

ZACETECAS

GDP in thousands of pesos:
10,937,468
Percent of GDP:
Manufacturing 11 percent
Commerce 55 percent
Service industries 34 percent
Per capita income: 8,095
Exports: Coffee, fresh fruits, fertilizer, sugar, fish & crustaceans.
Natural resources: gold, copper, silver, lead, zinc

PER CAPITA INCOME = the amount earned in an area divided by the total number of people living in that area
GDP = Gross Domestic Product, the total value of goods and services produced during the year
1 PESO = about $0.11, as of spring 2002

Figures from INEGI, the Mexican National Institute of Statistics, based on Mexico's 2000 census.

Three canyons meet near the town of Divasadero in the Sierra Tarahumara mountains of Chihuahua. Although the country was colonized by Spain in the 16th century, many of the native peoples, such as the Tarahumara and the Maya, have managed to keep their traditional culture alive.

THE CULTURE

The northern part of Mexico is much closer to the United States geographically and culturally. Much of what goes on in the towns is directed toward the border—the factories, the tourists who come and go. But outside of the cities, in places like the Sierra Tarahumara, the Indians live as they always have.

There are 50 to 70 thousand Rarahumari or Tarahumara living in the Copper Canyon in caves, under cliffs, and in small cabins. These people raise corn and beans and some animals. The name Rarahumurai means "running people" or "footrunners," and they are known for how fast they run barefoot up the mountains. They are famous for their nonstop, long-distance foot races that may last as long as 72 hours. The phrase they use to describe their running is "foot throwing." A game they like to play is known as Rariparo and involves teams kicking a wooden ball. These people live closely to the earth; they fashion their plows from the limbs of oak trees, and they are skilled in the preparation of more than 200 species of edible plants. They are determined to follow the ancient traditions of their ancestors; for centuries, they have successfully resisted all outside efforts to modernize their way of life.

42

When you travel from Copper Canyon to a city on the border like Ciudad Juárez, it is almost like traveling through time. The modern border towns have more in common with modern European or American cities than they do with the primitive villages of their own state.

Whether primitive or modern, however, like the rest of Mexico the people of the northern states love to celebrate. They enjoy festivals, fairs, feast days, national holidays, and religious holidays. Every town has its own saint and celebrates on that saint's special day. Local regions also have their own unique celebrations for the harvest of their particular crops. Most of these joyous events involve music, dancing, feasting, and fireworks.

Along with the rest of the nation, northern Mexico celebrates the following holidays:

* *Carnaval*, the Tuesday before the beginning of **Lent**, when people parade through the streets in costumes.
* *Holy Week*, from Palm Sunday to Easter Sunday.

	STATE POPULATION	GROWTH RATE
Chihuahua	3,052,907	2.3%
Coahuila	2,298,070	1.6%
Durango	1,448,661	0.7%
Nuevo León	3,834,141	2.2%
San Luis Potosí	2,299,360	1.4%
Tamaulipas	2,753,222	2.1%
Zacatecas	1,353,610	0.6%

Mexico's ethnic groups:
Indian-Spanish (mestizo): 60 percent
Indian: 30 percent
White: 9 percent
Other: 1 percent

Education: **12 years of education is required from ages 6 through 18. About 94 percent of school-age children are enrolled in school. The literacy rate is 89 percent.**

Mexico's religions:
Roman Catholic 89 percent
Protestant: 6 percent
Other 5 percent

Two Tarahumara girls use a stick to toss a hoop forward as part of a race. They are participating in games and dances in an effort to keep their traditional culture alive.

* *Cinco de Mayo*, May 5, when Mexicans celebrate their victory over France at the battle of Puebla in 1862.
* *Día de la Raza*, October 12 (Columbus Day in the United States), when Mexicans celebrate the mingling of races that makes their nation unique.
* *Día de los Muertos* (Day of the Dead), October 31-November 2, when Mexicans honor their dead with celebrations and feasting.
* *The Feast of the Virgin of Guadalupe*, December 12, when Mexicans honor their patron saint.
* Advent and Christmas, December 16-25, when Mexicans celebrate *Posado*, honoring Mary and Joseph's search for shelter, and then spend Christmas Day as a quiet religious holiday.

Various local cities and regions have their own celebrations as well. In Chihuahua, the Tarahumara people have incorporated the festivals of the Virgin of Guadalupe and *Semana Santa* (Holy Week)

A tourist studies the ruins of a brick building near Copper Canyon in Chihuahua. Tourism has been on the rise in Mexico since the 1970s, when Americans discovered its possibilities as a close, affordable, and beautiful vacation spot.

with their own religious traditions. They celebrate these occasions with elaborate costumes and dancing, honoring the sun, which is their symbol for God, the Mother and Father of their people.

From July 18 to August 3, people of Coahuila flood the streets of Saltillo to celebrate the annual *Feria de Saltillo*. This region was first settled by 400 Tlaxcalteca families, people who were craftsmakers and weavers by trade, and Saltillo's fair celebrates their descendants'

Carnaval stretches over five days, encompassing Mexico's celebration of the traditional holidays before Lent. Festivalgoers dress up and parade for Fat Tuesday and Ash Wednesday, as well as for lesser-known events such as the Day of the Oppressed Husband.

artistry and culture. Colorful woolen **serapes** are a symbol of these people's traditional lifestyle and unique culture.

Every July, Durango celebrates for two weeks. The festival starts July 4, the day of the *Virgen del Refugio*, and continues through July 22, the anniversary of Durango's founding in 1563. The celebration is known throughout Mexico, and people from all over the country come to buy cows, bet on cockfights, and enjoy the food, music, dancing, and rides.

Townsfolk costumed as skeletons carry a coffin through the streets in a mock funeral. Celebrations for the Day of the Dead may appear morbid to outsiders, but they carry a great deal of significance for Mexican participants.

Monterrey, the capital city of Nuevo León, has a very different annual event—a lottery. Every year thousands of hopeful people buy tickets for the national lottery sponsored by Monterrey's Technology Institute. The grand prize is a dream house, designed and built by experts chosen by the Institute. The prize also includes enough money to furnish the house—and an additional sum for upkeep for many years to come.

The people of San Luis Potosí celebrate the last two weeks of August. They flock to the capital city for the *Fiesta Nacional Potosina*. The festival

includes concerts, bullfights, fireworks, and a parade. The celebration of the city's patron saint, San Luis, also falls during this time.

Come May, the city will again celebrate for another 10 days. This time the *Festival de las Artes* will fill the city with music, dance, and theater performances.

The border towns of Tamaulipas are so close to Texas that the United States is a big influence on their culture. Everything tends to cater to the tourists who come in throngs looking for cheap handicrafts and after-dark thrills in the rough bars and cantinas that fill these cities. This area of Mexico is not famous for its food or drink—but many tourists do enjoy the buzz of caffeine they experience when they drink this region's traditional beverage: *café de olla*, a blend of coffee, chocolate, and cinnamon that is brewed slowly in a clay pot.

The people of Zacatecas sometimes celebrate a private **fiesta** called a *callejonada*. A donkey, with gallons of **mescal** on its back, strolls through the alleys and back streets of the capital city. Music and dancing follow along behind—and everyone is welcome to join the party.

The Rancho de las Golondrinas is now a living history museum. In the early 1700s, however, it was an important stop along the famous Camino Real, or Royal Road, from Mexico City to Santa Fe, New Mexico.

CITIES AND COMMUNITIES

Many of Mexico's most modern, wealthy, and industrialized cities lie opposite the United States along the northern border. Some Mexicans feel that the United States dominates Mexico, intruding where it doesn't belong. Many believe that U.S. businesses take advantage of the cheap labor of the Mexican workers.

In these northern cities are the *maquiladoras*—the factories that are often owned by companies from the United States. Here too people regularly go back and forth over the border into the United States, sometimes working in one country and living in the other. Perhaps more than in any other part of Mexico, people in the northern states' cities feel related to the United States. Indeed, they often have relations across the border.

Chihuahua City, with nearly a million people, is the 12th-largest city in Mexico and one of its most industrialized. Timber and mining concerns, as well *maquiladoras*, are based in Chihuahua, although the dog that takes its name from the city is rarely seen.

Originally settled by silver miners at the start of the 18th century, Chihuahua has served as a refuge for many political figures. Miguel Hidalgo fled here during the War of Independence, and here Benito Juárez lived during the Revolution. The city's most famous resident and greatest hero was the outlaw Pancho Villa. In the Museum of the Revolution you can see the car he was driving when he was assassinated in 1923. The car is just as he last saw it, bullet holes and all.

Since NAFTA, Ciudad Juárez has become a thriving city. Once known as Paso del Norte, Juárez marks the spot where Don Juan de Onate crossed the Río Grande. This occurred 60 years after the arrival of Cortés and 40 years before the Pilgrims came to Plymouth Rock. In 1668 Father Garcia de San Francisco founded the Mission of Our Lady of Guadelupe where mass is still said daily. Juárez served as an important way station along the Camino Real (Royal Road), and the cattle drivers would stop here to water their herds on the way to Texas. Some of its most famous inhabitants have included outlaws like Billy the Kid, John Wesley Hardin, and Pancho Villa. In 1856, Benito Juárez established his government here and the city was renamed in his honor.

The state of Chihuahua contains people as diverse as the land itself. In the 1920s, **Mennonites** from the United States were attracted here by the rich pastures, and today they still maintain their communities in Chihuahua's agricultural areas. Like the Mennonites, the Tarahumara people live in isolation from the rest of the world, but their ancient native culture is far different. The Tarahumara sell their crafts in Chihuahua's cities, and then retreat to their simple lifestyle in Chihuahua's Sierra Madres.

Two Mennonite men lean against a wall in a Mennonite settlement in Mexico, while a young boy scans the surrounding area. Mennonites from the United States moved into Mexico during the early 20th century, attracted by the fertile land as well as the opportunity to raise their families isolated from other cultures.

Saltillo, capital of Coahuila and the 21st largest city in Mexico, boasts walnut trees, vineyards, and pleasant temperatures. Once a cattle farming town, Saltillo's fresh climate has made it a pleasant stopping place. Saltillo is known for its colorful serapes.

Francisco de Ibarra founded the city of Durango in 1564 and named it after his hometown in Spain. In 1616 Durango was the scene of a bloody Indian rebellion where 15,000 people died. Today, much of Durango's wealth comes out of one of the largest iron deposits in the world, under the mountain Cerro de Mercado. You may have seen the city of Durango a thousand times in the Western movies that were filmed here. Such film stars as John Wayne and Paul Newman have come here to star in Westerns that were filmed in the spectacular desert scenery.

A poster advertising a bullfight in Monterrey is displayed on a public wall. Many Mexicans are passionate about keeping their culture alive through customs and traditions.

Monterrey, the capital city and the third largest city in Mexico, is called the "Pittsburgh of Mexico" because of the many mills that convert the country's iron and coal reserves into steel. Monterrey is the major center of the Mexican steel industry—and it is also known for its 20 colleges. *Fortune* magazine voted Monterrey the best city in Latin America for business. With air conditioning, modern building, and shopping malls, it would be hard to distinguish Monterrey from any large city in the United States. Eighty-five percent of Nuevo León's population lives here in this modern city. Three thousand trucks pass through daily on their way to and from Texas.

Despite Monterrey's industrial wealth, the city has a reputation throughout Mexico as being a place where stingy people live. In fact,

This statue of Father Miguel Hidalgo stands in the middle of a village plaza. Following Mexico's Independence Day, this statue will be adorned with red, white, and green flowers to acknowledge Hidalgo's influence in the fight for a free Mexico.

they're thought to be so tight-fisted that if you want to order a glass of ice water in a Mexican restaurant, just ask for "A Monterrey on the rocks."

In the 17th century, the city of San Luis Potosí, the state's present-day capital, was the capital of Northern New Spain. It was also home to Juárez, and here he signed the death sentence of the Emperor Maximilian. Today San Luis Potosí calls itself Ciudad de los Jardines, the city of gardens, because of its many parks. Overall, though, this is an industrial city with factories, and a few well-preserved old buildings.

Matamoros, directly across the border from Brownsville, Texas, boasts the Museum of Corn as well as a fort left from the Mexican-American War. Matamoros also has a significant Jewish population, since Jewish families from the center of Mexico settled here in the early 20th century to avoid religious persecution. The first *maquiladora* in Mexico was built here, and

Benito Pablo Juárez was born to Zapotec Indian parents in Oaxaca. He went on to twice be elected president of his country. His main goal was to apply some degree of reform to the tumultuous government of Mexico.

today there are 120 of these factories. With 490,000 residents, Matamoros is the 15th-largest city in Mexico.

Nuevo Laredo is located in the state of Tamaulipas on the border of Mexico and the United States. This city was founded in 1755 when Laredo, Texas, became part of the United States. At that time, some Mexican people crossed to the south of the Río Grande to establish a "new" Laredo, because they wanted to remain Mexicans. Between 1950 and 1995, Nuevo Laredo has grown nearly five times over. Currently, it has a population of slightly over 350,000, and it has been projected to grow to over 400,000 residents in the next few years.

Tampico, a bustling port town in Tamaulipas, has a population of 313,400 and is the 44th-largest city in the country. The largest city in

Tamaulipas, Tampico was first settled by Huastec Indians and then by the Aztecs. Today, Tampico is still famous for an incident between Mexico and the United States that occurred in 1914. The United States captured the port, helping the rebels overthrow President Huerta.

The city of Zacetecas, the capital of the state, winds like a maze built in between and on top of steep hills. The buildings at the center of town are built from a rosy sandstone, which makes the city seem brightly pink. It was once a prosperous silver town, and it still supplies 34 percent of Mexico's silver. The beautiful Templo de Santo Domingo, filled with ornate golden decoration, was built between 1730 and 1760; it represents of a style of architecture for which Mexico is famous—Churrigueresque. Named for Jose Churriguera, a Spanish architect, this style is extravagant and fancy; it combined elements of both Spanish and native Mexican architecture.

As you travel from one of these cities to the next, it is impossible not to be struck by the history that lives in each of them. The past and present lie in layers, from modern skyscrapers to ancient churches. The echoes of **Nahuatl**, Spanish, and English voices come together in an exciting symphony.

Mexico's cities' greatest strength has always come from their people—their unique culture, their creativity, and their faith. The problems handed down from past centuries are still visible in these cities' poverty—but as the Mexican people work with a new administration, who knows how the northern states will grow in the century to come?

CHRONOLOGY

150 B.C.	Teotihuacán is built.
A.D. 750	Teotihuacán is abandoned.
300–900	Peak cultural growth of the Maya.
	Aztecs begin to conquer other tribes for control of Mexico.
1325	Aztecs build Tenochtitlán.
1500	Aztecs control all land in central Mexico.
1519	Hernán Cortés arrives in central Mexico.
1521	Spanish take control of Mexico.
1810	Father Miguel Hidalgo calls for Mexico's independence from Spain.
1821	Mexico wins its independence.
1845	The Mexican-American War begins.
1854	Benito Juárez becomes president of Mexico.
1862	France invades Mexico.
1867	Juárez triumphs over the French, executes the Emperor Maximilian, and resumes his presidency.
1876	Porfirio Díaz begins his period of dictatorship.
1910–1921	The Mexican Revolution.
1968	Mexico hosts the Summer Olympic Games, and violence breaks out during a student protest.
2000	Vicente Fox becomes president and vows to improve his nation's economy and social inequality.
2001	President Fox meets with U.S. President George W. Bush to discuss a cooperative relationship between the neighboring countries.
2002	Latin American leaders, including Mexico's Vicente Fox, meet in Argentina for the Global Alumni Conference to discuss technological and economic issues.

FOR MORE INFORMATION

CHIHUAHUA

Government of Chihuahua
http://www.chihuahua.gob.mx

State Tourism Office
Calle Libertad No. 1300
Edif. Agustin Melgar, 1 Piso
CP 31000 Chihuahua, Chih.
Tel: (14) 29-3421
Fax: (14) 16-0032
E-mail:
cturismo@buzon.chihuahua.gob.mx

COAHUILA

Government of Coahuila
http://www.coahuila.gob.mx

State Tourism Office
Blvd. Luis Echeverría No. 1560
Edif. Torre Saltillo Piso 11
CP 25286 Saltillo, Coah.
Tel: (84) 15-2162
Fax: (84) 15-2174

DURANGO

Government of Durango
http://www.durango.gob.mx

State Tourism Office
Hidalgo No. 408 Sur
CP 34000 Durango, Dgo.
Tel: (18) 11-3160
Fax: (18) 11-9677

NUEVO LEÓN

Government of Nuevo León
http://www.nuevoleon.gob.mx

State Tourism Office
Zaragoza No. 1300 Sur
Edif. Kalos Nivel A-1 Desp. 137
CP64000 Monterrey, N.L.
Tel: (8) 344-4343
Fax: (8) 344-1169
E-mail: info@mty-mex-travel.com

FOR MORE INFORMATION

SAN LUIS POTOSÍ

Government of San Luis Potosí
http://www.slp.gob.mx

State Tourism Office
Alvaro Obregón No. 520
CP 78000 San Luis Potosí, S.L.P.
Tel: (48) 12-9939
Fax: (48) 12-6769

TAMAULIPAS

Government of Tamaulipas
http://www.tamaulipas.gob.mx

State Tourism Office
16 Rosales No. 272
CP 87000 Cd. Victoria, Tamps.
Tel: (131) 2-1057
Fax: (131) 2-7002

ZACATECAS

Government of Zacatecas
http://www.zacatecas.gob.mx

State Tourism Office
Prol. González Ortega y Esteban
Castorena s/n
CP 98000 Zacatecas, Zac.
Tel: (492) 4-0052
Fax: (492) 2-9329

THINGS TO DO AND SEE

CHIHUAHUA

Copper Canyon

Cerocahui's Tarahumar dances and Jesuit mission

Sangre de Cristo gold mines

COAHUILA

La Cascada de Caballo (Horsetail Falls), a dramatic waterfall

Saltillo's cultural center

DURANGO

Regional Museum of Durango, containing fossils and mummies

The city of Durango's Palacio de Gobierno, a baroque palace that houses two of Mexico's great 20th-century murals, one by Francisco Montoya and the other by Ernesto Flores Esquivel

NUEVO LEÓN

Parque de los Niños Heroes (Park of the Child Heroes), which also contains several museums

SAN LUIS POTOSÍ

Santa María del Río, a village famous for its handcrafted silk and cotton shawls. These techniques originated in Asia centuries ago, were passed to Spain during the Moors' invasion, and then were brought to Mexico by the conquistadors.

Real de Catorce, a ghost town

TAMAULIPAS

The beaches of Tampico

El Cielo Nature Preserve

ZACATECAS

The aqueduct of the city of Zacatecas

Cerro de la Bufa (Hill of the Wineskin), a hill that allows a magnificent view of the surrounding landscape; a museum, chapel, and cemetery are also on the hill

Eden Mine, which operated from the 1500s until 1964

FURTHER READING

Burke, Michael E. *Hippocrene Companion Guide to Mexico*. New York: Hippocrene Books, 1992.

Coe, Michael D. Coe. *Mexico*. New York: Thames and Hudson, 1994.

Collis, John and David M. Jones (Eds.). *Blue Guide Mexico*. New York: Norton, 1997.

Fodor's Mexico 2001. New York: Fodor's Travel Publications, 2001.

Let's Go: Mexico. New York: Let's Go, Inc., 2001.

Mexico Travel Book. Tampa, Fla.: AAA Publishing, 2000.

Wilcock, John, Kal Muller, and Martha Ellen Zenfell (Eds.). *Insight Guides, Mexico*. New York: Langenscheidt Publishers, 1998.

INTERNET RESOURCES

INEGI (Geographic, Demographic, and Economic Information of Mexico)
http://www.inegi.gob.mx/diffusion/ingles/portadai.html

Mesoweb
http://www.mesoweb.com/welcome.html#externalresources

Mexico for Kids
http://www.elbalero.gob.mx/index_kids.html

Mexico Channel
http://www.mexicochannel.net

GLOSSARY

Aqueducts	Bridge-like structures that carry water pipes.
Cabinet	An advisory council to the head of a government.
Cisterns	An underground tank for storing drinking water.
Conquistadors	Spanish conquerors of the New World.
Exported	Shipped goods or services out of a country.
Fiesta	Spanish party or celebration.
Haciendas	Large Mexican ranches.
Immunities	The body's abilities to resist certain diseases.
Imported	Brought goods or services into a country.
Interest rates	The percent at which loans and savings increase.
Irrigated	Brought water to the land by artificial means.
Lent	The six weeks before Easter, a time of fasting and repentance.
Jesuit	A member of the Roman Catholic Society of Jesus, founded by St. Ignatius Loyala in 1534 and devoted to missionary and educational work.
Mennonites	Members of a Protestant religious group who believe in pacifism and sometime isolate themselves from the influences of modern society.
Mescal	A colorless Mexican liquor distilled from the leaves of maguey plants.
Migrate	To move from one region to another.
Nahuatl	The ancient language spoken by the Aztecs; still spoken by many modern Mexicans.
Petition	A formal written request, usually signed by many people.
Plateau	High, level land.
Serapes	Colorful woolen shawls worn by Mexican men.
Vaqueros	Mexican cowboys.

THE STATES OF NORTHERN MEXICO

INDEX

PICTURE CREDITS

2:	©OTTN Publishing	35:	Phil Schermeister/Corbis
3:	IMS Communications, Ltd.	36:	Eye Ubiquitous/Corbis
10:	Phil Schermeister/Corbis	40:	Macduff Everton/Corbis
13:	David A. Northcott/Corbis	43:	Phil Schermeister/Corbis
14:	George H. H. Huey/Corbis	44:	Phil Schermeister/Corbis
15:	IMS Communications, Ltd.	45:	Liba Taylor/Corbis
16:	Macduff Everton/Corbis	46:	Reuters NewMedia Inc./Corbis
20:	IMS Communications, Ltd.	48:	Dave G. House/Corbis
23:	IMS Communications, Ltd.	51:	Bettmann/Corbis
24:	Hulton/Archive	52:	IMS Communications, Ltd.
25:	Corbis	53:	Danny Lehman/Corbis
26:	Reuters NewMedia Inc./Corbis	54:	Hulton/Archive
30:	Macduff Everton/Corbis		
33:	IMS Communications, Ltd.	Cover	(front) IMS Communications, Ltd.
34:	Nik Wheeler/Corbis		(inset) IMS Communications, Ltd.
			(back) IMS Communications, Ltd.

CONTRIBUTORS

Roger E. Hernández is the most widely syndicated columnist writing on Hispanic issues in the United States. His weekly column, distributed by King Features, appears in some 40 newspapers across the country, including the *Washington Post*, *Los Angeles Daily News*, *Dallas Morning News*, *Arizona Republic*, *Rocky Mountain News* in Denver, *El Paso Times*, and *Hartford Courant*. He is also the author of *Cubans in America*, an illustrated history of the Cuban presence in what is now the United States, from the early colonists in 16th-century Florida to today's Castro-era exiles. The book was designed to accompany a PBS documentary of the same title.

Hernández's articles and essays have been published in the *New York Times*, *New Jersey Monthly*, *Reader's Digest*, and *Vista Magazine*; he is a frequent guest on television and radio political talk shows, and often travels the country to lecture on his topic of expertise. Currently, he is teaching journalism and English composition at the New Jersey Institute of Technology in Newark, where he holds the position of writer-in-residence. He is also a member of the adjunct faculty at Rutgers University.

Hernández left Cuba with his parents at the age of nine. After living in Spain for a year, the family settled in Union City, New Jersey, where Hernandez grew up. He attended Rutgers University, where he earned a BA in Journalism in 1977; after graduation, he worked in television news before moving to print journalism in 1983. He lives with his wife and two children in Upper Montclair, New Jersey.

AUTHOR

Deirdre Day-MacLeod is a freelance writer. She lives in Montclair, New Jersey. She is also the author of *The States of Central Mexico*.

St. Helena Library

P9-BIC-598

ST. HELENA PUBLIC LIBRARY
1492 LIBRARY LANE
ST. HELENA, CA 94574-1143
(707) 963-5244

OUR
SOUTHERN NEIGHBOR
MEXICO

THE PACIFIC SOUTH STATES OF MEXICO

SHERYL NANTUS

24°N

Gulf of
Mexico

22°N

MEXICO

20°N

Bay of Compeche

Colima
COLIMA

18°N

GUERRERO
Chilpancingo

Oaxaca
OAXACA

CHIAPAS
Tuxtla Gutiérrez

Acapulco

16°N

*Gulf of
Tehuantepec*

N

W ← → E

S

GUATEMALA

14°N

| 0 | 100 | 200 Miles |
| 0 | 100 | 200 Kilometers |

Albers Conic Equal-Area Projection

12°N

PACIFIC OCEAN

10°N

104°W   102°W   100°W   98°W   96°W   94°W   92°W

2/04

J972

THE PACIFIC SOUTH STATES OF MEXICO

SHERYL NANTUS

Mason Crest Publishers
Philadelphia

Mason Crest Publishers
370 Reed Road
Broomall PA 19008
www.masoncrest.com

Copyright © 2003 by Mason Crest Publishers. All rights reserved.

First printing

1 3 5 7 9 8 6 4 2

Library of Congress Cataloging-in-Publication Data

Nantus, Sheryl.
  States of the Pacific South of Mexico / by Sheryl Nantus.
    p.   cm. — (Mexico: Our Southern Neighbor)
    Includes bibliographical references and index.
Summary: Provides information on the geography, history, economy, culture,
  and cities and communities of the states along Mexico's Pacific coast.
    ISBN 1-59084-084-4 (hc.)
1. Mexico – Juvenile literature. 2. Pacific Coast (Mexico)–Juvenile literature.
[1. Pacific Coast (Mexico) 2. Mexico.] I. Title. II. Series.
F1208.5.N36 2002
972—dc21
                                                              2001052218

TABLE OF CONTENTS

OUR SOUTHERN NEIGHBOR MEXICO

Roger E. Hernández
Senior Consulting Editor

INTRODUCTION

exico is a country in the midst of great change. And what happens in Mexico will have an important impact on the United States, its neighbor to the north.

These changes are being put in place by President Vicente Fox, who was elected in 2000. For the previous 71 years, power had been held by presidents from one single party, known in Spanish as *Partido Revolucionario Institucional* (Institutional Revolutionary Party, or PRI). Some of those presidents have been accused of corruption. President Fox, from a different party called *Partido de Acción Nacional* (National Action Party, or PAN), says he wants to eliminate that corruption. He also wants to have a friendlier relationship with the United States, and for American businesses to increase trade with Mexico. That will create more jobs, he says, and decrease poverty—which in turn will mean fewer Mexicans will find themselves forced to emigrate in search of a better life.

But it would be wrong to think of Mexico as nothing more than a poor country. Mexico has given the world some of its greatest artists and writers. Carlos Fuentes is considered one of the greatest living novelists, and poet-essayist Octavio Paz was awarded the Nobel Prize for Literature in 1990, the most prestigious honor a writer can win. Painters such as Diego Rivera and José Clemente Orozco specialized in murals, huge paintings done on walls that tell of the history of the nation. Another famous Mexican painter, Rufino Tamayo, blended the "cubist" style of modern European painters like Picasso with native folk themes.

Tamayo's paintings in many ways symbolize what Mexico is: A blend of the culture of Europe (more specifically, its Spanish version) and the indigenous cultures that predated the arrival of Columbus.

Those cultures were thriving even 3,000 years ago, when the Olmec people built imposing monuments that survive to this day in what are now the states of Tabasco and Veracruz. Later and further to the south in the Yucatán Peninsula, the Maya civilization flourished. They constructed cities in the midst of the jungle, complete with huge temples, courts in which ball games were played, and highly accurate calendars intricately carved in stone pillars. For some mysterious reason, the Mayans abandoned most of these great centers 1,100 years ago.

The Toltecs, in central Mexico, were the next major civilization. They were followed by the Aztecs. It was the Aztecs who built the city of Tenochitlán in the middle of a lake in what is now Mexico City, with long causeways connecting it to the mainland. By the early 1500s it was one of the largest cities anywhere, with perhaps 200,000 inhabitants.

Then the Spanish came. In 1519, twenty-seven years after Columbus arrived in the Americas, Hernán Cortés landed in Yucatán with just 600 soldiers plus a few cannons and horses. They marched inland, gaining allies as they went along among indigenous peoples who resented being ruled by the Aztecs. Within two years Cortés and the Spaniards ruled Mexico. They had conquered the Aztec Empire and devastated their great capital.

It was in that destruction that modern Mexico was born. The influence of the Aztecs and other indigenous people did not disappear even though untold numbers were killed. But neither can Mexico be recognized today without the Spanish influence.

Spain ruled for three centuries. Then in 1810 Mexicans began a struggle for independence from colonial Spain, much like the United States had fought for its own independence from Great Britain. In 1821 Mexico finally became an independent nation.

The newly born republic faced many difficulties. There was much poverty, especially among descendants of indigenous peoples; most of the wealth and political power was in the hands of a small elite of Spanish ancestry. To make things worse, Mexico lost almost half of its territory to the United States in a war that lasted from 1846 to 1848. Many still resent the loss of territory, which accounts for lingering anti-American sentiments among some Mexicans. The country was later occupied by France, but under national hero Benito Juárez Mexico regained its independence in 1867.

The next turning point in Mexican history came in 1911, when a revolution meant to help the millions of Mexicans stuck in poverty began against dictator Porfirio Díaz. There was violence and fighting until 1929, when Plutarco Elías Calles founded what was to become the *Partido Revolucionario Institucional*. It brought stability as well as economic progress. Yet millions of Mexicans remained in poverty, and as time went on PRI rulers became increasingly corrupt.

It was the desire of the people of Mexico to trust someone other than the candidate of PRI that resulted in the election of Fox. And so this nation of more than 100 million, with its ancient heritage, its diverse mestizo culture, its grinding poverty, and its glorious arts, stands on the brink of a new era. Modern Mexico is seeking a place as the leader of all Latin America, an ally of the United States, and an important voice in global politics. For that to happen, Mexico must narrow the gap between the rich and poor and bring more people in the middle class. It will be interesting to watch as Fox and the Mexican people work to bring their country into the first rank of nations.

THE LAND

Mexico's Pacific South is a land rich in history and natural resources. These states—Colima, Guerrero, Oaxaca, Chiapas—are a diverse mixture of mountains and tropical vegetation. They are sometimes shaken by earthquakes and volcanoes, or tossed and flooded by hurricanes, but their beauty remains.

Colima is one of the smallest states in Mexico, with only 2,106 square miles (5,455 square kilometers) in total, only 0.3 percent of Mexico's total land. But this small area has a great variety of environments within it, from warm and humid temperatures at an average 78 degrees Fahrenheit (26 degrees Celsius) in the Armeria River valley near the center of the state, to a brisker 62 degrees Fahrenheit (17 degrees Celsius) in the higher altitudes to the northwest. The coast of Colima is at the latitude of 19 degrees north, the same as Jamaica and Hawaii.

Between December and February you can find the coolest temperatures for this area, although nothing like the North American winter. The weather is warm for most of the rest of the year, with the

There is beautiful scenery throughout mountainous Chiapas, including the steep walls of the Canyon de Sumidero in Tuxtla Gutierrez.

rainy season running between June and October; providing needed moisture to the forest after the hot and humid months of July and August. Unfortunately, the rainy season is also the hurricane season, a major concern for many. While Colima was badly hit by Hurricane Pauline in October of 1997, the nearby states of Guerrero and Oaxaca were hit much harder, with over 200 deaths and major destruction of property.

Colima is surrounded on three sides by Jalisco and by Michoacán to the southeast. Directly south of Colima is the Pacific Ocean, where the Revillagigedo Archipelago lies, part of Colima as well. Although it is one of the smallest states in Mexico, Colima has some of the most varied geographical features. Starting at the many beaches on the Pacific Coast, the land rises up to the rich farms that dot the countryside. At the northeastern tip of the state, two volcanoes tower over the small villages—and one of them is still quite active!

Sitting right at the southernmost edge of Mexico is Chiapas, the eighth largest state in the country. Consisting of 28,732 square miles (74,416 square kilometers), its boundaries run along the Pacific Ocean to the south to the border with Guatemala in the east and then north to the state of Tabasco, with Oaxaca and Veracruz bordering it to the west.

Going inward from the coast, you immediately find yourself climbing the Sierra Madre de Chiapas, a large mountain range running parallel to the ocean. These mountains reach up to 13,310 feet (4,057 meters), with the spectacular Tacana Volcano just inside the Guatemala border. Moving inland, you find the lush river valley of the Grijalva and northeast of them the central highlands, with lower lakes and valleys feeding into the Usumacinta River and eventually into Tabasco. Most of

Mayan boys swim through the streets after Hurricane Roxanne flooded their town in 1995. Hurricanes and tropical storms are always a danger in the Pacific south states of Mexico.

the forest is made up of valuable *dyewoods* and hardwoods, making it both an economic and cultural treasure, as more and more discussion arises about how to both preserve the forests and harvest the benefits of the land for the people. Two of the most popular woods harvested here are *mahogany* and *rosewood*.

The climate of Chiapas varies from area to area. In the north part of the state you can find very dry hot weather, varying greatly from the southern parts where the humidity makes the air feel hotter than the actual temperature. The average temperature is 68 degrees Fahrenheit (20 degrees Celsius), with some measurements going as high as 104 degrees Fahrenheit (40 degrees Celsius) and as low as 32 degrees Fahrenheit (0 degrees Celsius). The rainy season runs from June to November. Needless to say, if you visit Chiapas, you better prepare for all types of weather.

Located on the Pacific Coast, Guerrero has one of Mexico's most famous cities in its midst—Acapulco. With a surface area of 24,818 miles (64,282 square kilometers), this state has only 3.3 percent of Mexico's land area, but that includes 313 miles (500 kilometers) of coastline. The Sierra Madre del Sur runs southwest just inside the coastline, cresting at 12,149 feet (3,703 meters). Bordered to the north and west by Michoacán; Oaxaca to the east and southeast; Puebla to the northeast; and Morelos to the northwest, Guerrero occupies a small but important position in Mexico past and present.

The main river running through the area is called the Río de las Balsas, beginning at the northwest tip of the state and running almost directly down the center, with smaller rivers branching off until it meets Oaxaca at the other end of the state. Because of the moisture available

The western Sierra Madre mountain range, which runs through Chiapas, Guerrero, and Oaxaca, features a great variety of lush vegetation.

A plume of ash rises from the top of a volcano that erupted in 1991 near the border between Colima and Jalisco.

and the temperatures that can vary from a high of over 90 degrees Fahrenheit (32 degrees Celsius) to a low of 80 degrees Fahrenheit (26 degrees Celsius), the climate is hot and rainy on the coastlines. On the highlands further inland, near the center of the Mexican peninsula, the climate balances out enough so crops can be grown and harvested.

Oaxaca is found in the southwest area of Mexico, with the Pacific Ocean to the south. It shares borders with Guerrero, Chiapas, Puebla, and Veracruz. With a surface area of 94,211 square miles (244,007 square kilometers), Oaxaca is one of the five largest states of Mexico,

THE PACIFIC SOUTH STATES OF MEXICO

A church partially buried by the eruption of Paricutin, a volcano in the region. The States of Mexico's Pacific coast are part of the "ring of fire," a circle of active volcanoes.

with 4.85 percent of the nation's total surface area. Sitting along the mountains and valleys of the Tehuantepec Isthmus, this large state has a tropical climate resulting in massive amounts of rainfall throughout the land. Almost totally encircled by the Sierra Madre del Sur mountain range, the Oaxaca *plateau* contains extremely fertile land and is well suited to farming and agriculture. It produces sugarcane, coffee, and tobacco, among other crops.

The Isthmus of Tehuantepec is the name given to the narrowest piece of land in North America—as you can see on a map, it is extremely narrow and just barely separates the Pacific and Atlantic Oceans. Historically, this was an invaluable resource to travelers looking to avoid going all the way around the tip of South America; it was eagerly sought by traders and explorers alike.

With almost 316 miles (500 kilometers) of coastline, Oaxaca is poised to become a major tourist-based state, like its other nearby sister states. Until recently the beaches were ignored, but thanks to a series of government initiatives, such places as the Bahias de Huatulco project are appearing on tourist maps and destinations.

COLIMA

Location: Colima is surrounded on three sides by Jalisco and by Michoacán to the southeast. Directly south of Colima is the Pacific Ocean, where the Revillagigedo Archipelago lies, which is part of Colima as well.

Capital: Colima

Total Area: 2,106 square miles (5,455 square kilometers) in total; 103 miles (166 kilometers) of coastline.

Climate: Warm and humid with an average temperature of 78 degrees Fahrenheit (26 degrees Celsius).

Terrain: Nearly three quarters of Colima consists of mountains and hills.

Elevation: Fuego de Colima rises into the sky at 14,220 feet (4,323 meters) and Volcan de Fuego is 13,087 feet (3,980 meters) of live, active volcano.

Natural Hazards: Volcanoes; hurricanes.

CHIAPAS

Location: Sitting right at the southernmost edge of Mexico is Chiapas, the eighth largest State in the country. Its boundaries run along the Pacific Ocean to the south to the border with Guatemala in the east and then north to the state of Tabasco, with Oaxaca and Veracruz bordering it to the west.

Capital: Tuxtla Gutierrez

Total Area: 28,732 square miles (74,416 square kilometers), with over 173 miles (280 kilometers) of coastline.

Climate: The average temperature is 68 degrees Fahrenheit (20 degrees Celsius) with some measurements going as high as 104 degrees Fahrenheit (40 degrees Celsius) and as low as 32 degrees Fahrenheit (0 degrees Celsius). The rainy season runs from June to November.

Terrain: Going inward from the coast, you immediately find yourself climbing the Sierra Madre de Chiapas, a large mountain range running parallel to the ocean.

Elevation: The highest point in Chiapas is 13,310 feet (4,057 meters) at the Sierra Madre de Chiapas, with the lowest points being at sea level along the coastline.

Natural Hazards: Flooding.

GUERRERO

Location: Sitting on the Pacific Coast to the south of Michocán and bordered by Oaxaca ot the east and southeast and Puebla to the northeast, with Morelos to the northwest.

Capital: Chilpancingo

Total Area: 24,887 square miles (64,457 square kilometers)

Climate: Hot and rainy with temperatures ranging from 79 degrees Fahrenheit (26 degrees Celsius) on the coast to a cooler 59 degrees Fahrenheit (15 degrees Celsius) in the highlands where the land is drier and easier to farm.

Terrain: Mountainous throughout the state except for along the coastline.

Elevation: Rising from sea level on the coastline, the Sierra Madre del Sur reaches heights of well over 12,000 feet (3,000 meters) with notable mountains being Cero La Cruz at 7,250 feet (2,210 meters) and Cerro Baul at 10,215 feet (3,114 meters).

Natural Hazards: Hurricanes and earthquakes.

OAXACA

Location: Just north of the state of Chiapas, Oaxaca lies on the Pacific Ocean with the state of Veracruz to the north.

Capital: Oaxaca

Total Area: 36,375 square miles (94,211 square kilometers)

Climate: Tropical in the interior; hot and dry on the coast. Average temperatures are approximately 84 degrees Fahrenheit (29 degrees Celsius).

Terrain: Valleys dominate in the southern area with plateaus rising in the north to provide fertile farmland.

Elevation: The Sierra de Oaxaca has peaks as high as 10,000 feet.

Natural Hazards: Earthquakes.

An ancient stone temple stands in Palenque, Chiapas. Mayan remains such as this can be seen throughout the region.

THE HISTORY

Before the coming of the Spanish, Colima first came into its own as the Tecos Indians solidified their hold on the area. When they conquered the local area, they ensured that the kingdom of Colima became one of the most important parts of the ancient Chimalhuacana Confederation. But as the Spanish ***conquistadors*** swept across the country, Colima soon became a part of their new empire; the capital city of Colima was founded in 1523 by Gonzalo de Sandoval. Cortés, the famous explorer and conquistador, even appointed his nephew mayor of the city a few years later, hoping that the seaport would make Colima a valuable ***asset*** to the Spanish throne. But the Spanish king decided that Acapulco would make a better seaport and left Colima alone. As time went on, more and more land was added to Colima, resulting in a larger coastal presence. It became more important to the travelers going up and down the coastline, seeking safe harbors and trading posts. President Porfirio Díaz built a railroad across the small state to the new city of Manzanillo in the 1800s, making it a vital port of call for many ships.

In the early 20th century, during the Mexican Revolution, Colima suffered greatly, changing hands as the battles raged back and forth across its fertile lands. Slowly, though, the mining and shipping industries grew—and then the tourism industry grew and prospered as travelers discovered the beautiful beaches and allure of the still-active volcano.

The name comes from the Nahuatl language of the Aztecs, and it meant "old kingdom" or "domain of the lord." Literally, Colima was the "place conquered by our grandfathers"—or the "place dominated or ruled by the Fire God," a reference to the volcanoes nearby on the border between Colima and Jalisco.

The name Chiapas actually comes from two Nahuatl words, "Chia" and "Apan," meaning "in the river." Many people have lived in this area for as far back as there is recorded history, among them the Maya and the Aztecs. Many Mayan ruins dot the countryside, providing a great opportunity for archeologists to study this lost civilization. Many of these cities include pyramids, as well as drainage systems, huge statues, and intricate artwork centuries ahead of other civilizations at that time in Europe.

But the arrival of the Spanish in the 1500s meant the death of this civilization as the conquistadors raged across the countryside, plundering and attacking the inhabitants as well as introducing deadly diseases such as *smallpox* into the environment. The Maya had already begun to move away from their large cities, dispersing into small villages in the region, and the Spanish took very little note of them as they ransacked the area, searching for gold and precious metals. As the invaders set up their local governments, they left most native people

The Spanish conquistador Hernán Cortés meets the Aztec emperor Montezuma in this 19th-century illustration. The arrival of the Spaniards in the early 16th century forever changed life in Mexico.

alone and concentrated on collecting taxes and creating plantations to grow coffee and sugar. However, the Spanish experienced a high rate of failure in this region, due to the *malaria* and other diseases in the area that drained their labor force. Many Maya kept away from the Spanish, keeping to their small villages and creating their own societies where interaction with their invaders was kept to a minimum.

At this time, Chiapas was recognized as a province of Guatemala, not Mexico. Lacking the natural resources of the other areas to the north, Chiapas became a strategic worry for Spain as it tried to keep its hold

El Nevado, the "volcano of fire," is located on the border of Colima. The state got its name from the many volcanoes in the region.

on its conquests in the midst of losing its other territories. Attempts at farming continued, with the Indians being forced into labor under Spanish rule. This led to constant conflict between the Native Americans and the Spanish as each side tried to gain the upper hand.

Mexico, Guatemala, and the rest of the Spanish-conquered territories gained their independence in 1821. For another two years, Chiapas remained the property of Guatemala. Then, the citizens voted to join Mexico on September 14, 1824. This date is still celebrated all over Chiapas as the Día de la Mexicanidad or Day of Mexicanization. In 1892, the capital of Chiapas was moved from San Christóbal to Tuxtla Gutiérrez.

Unfortunately, in the last decade violence has marred the face of Chiapas. In 1994, several towns were occupied by rebels who wanted more independence for all of Mexico's native communities. Computer hackers have gotten involved with the Zapatista rebels also, sabotaging Mexican government sites since 1998 and attempting to overload the servers. With the new government elected in 2000, communication has improved dramatically between the rebels and President Vicente Fox's officials, leading to increased hope of a peaceful resolution for all parties involved.

Currently Chiapas is known as the home state of President Vicente Fox, with San Christóbal coming into the spotlight as his hometown. The state is at the forefront of his political effort to bring Mexico firmly into the 21st century, with economic and political changes aimed at improving conditions for everyone.

Like much of Mexico, Guerrero was the site of many ancient civilizations, with much activity concentrated on the coast. One such place was Zihuatanejo, not far from Ixtapa. Archeological digs in this area discovered stone carvings and figurines dating as far back as 3000 B.C., when the Olmecs were known to be in the area.

The original natives of Oaxaca included the Miztec, who built this compound hundreds of years ago.

This carved mask depicts a Mayan fire god. The Mayan civilization was in decline by the time the Spanish arrived in the 16th century, but descendants of the Mayans still live throughout the country today.

Like most other areas conquered by the Spanish, Guerrero suffered under the rule of the invaders for centuries, while being exploited as a source of natural resources. Its valuable seaports offered easy access to the wealth of the Mexican interior.

Unfortunately, this area was also the site of some of the heaviest fighting in the Mexican war for independence, weakening the local *infrastructure* even more in the early 1800s. Even after the Spanish disappeared from the scene, the state known as Guerrero did not exist until 1849; the land was divided up between the states of Michoacán, Puebla, and Oaxaca. But pressure from the local inhabitants who wanted control over their own land and an urge to remember Vicente Guerrero, the president who put an end to slavery in Mexico, resulted in the state being created.

A small antigovernment faction emerged in the late 1990s, not unlike those in Chiapas. This faction demanded more local control and independence from Mexico. At present, its influence has been small, and the Mexican army has contained the faction's forces. Time will tell if this newest move for independence will be resurrected.

The area known now as Oaxaca was home to many local tribes thousands of years ago. These tribes built such archeological wonders as Monte Albán, Mitla, and Yagul. At first the Zapotec and Miztec civilizations ruled this area. When the Aztecs invaded in the 15th century they absorbed the other tribes and gave Oaxaca its name. In the Nahuatl language, Oaxaca means "by the acacia grove."

When the Spanish invaded, Oaxaca fell to the conquistadors. As a reward, the Spanish king gave Cortés the official title of Marquis of the Oaxaca Valley. Cortés never settled in the area, but until the early 1900s his descendants held title to the land.

In the 20th century, Oaxaca has been prominent in politics. Two presidents have come from this area—Benito Juárez, the first full-blooded Indian to become a head of state, and Porfirio Díaz, who ruled Mexico for more than 30 years. Díaz constructed railways and encouraged modernization, but he was removed from power in 1911, when revolutionaries plunged the country into civil war.

Since then Oaxaca has struggled to maintain its infrastructure and to improve itself. To help the state achieve this goal, the government has made massive investments in the tourist industry on the coastline.

A colorful display of fresh fruit at Mercado Central, the bustling main market of Acapulco.

THE ECONOMY

The Pacific South, like much of Mexico, is very poor. However, rich natural resources and growing industries provide hope for the future.

Over the years Colima has developed a reputation as a leading producer of lemons, providing more than 60 percent of the domestic market. Bananas and coconuts are close behind, as well as corn, rice, and mangos. Constant improvements to the land through techniques such as irrigation will increase production of these popular foods. Other industries have also moved in, such as processing plants for cotton, rice, and corn (maize), as well as salt refining and manufacturing leather goods. Beverage production and clothing production are also major industries. As a result, the manufacturing industry has over 600 industrial plants in this rather small state. The recent discovery of iron ore has encouraged the development of processing plants, with the result that Colima is now one of Mexico's largest iron-producing states. The port of Manzanillo, which handles both domestic and international shipping, has gained major importance as a hub for trade with the United States and the countries of Central and South America, as well as countries across the Pacific Ocean.

On the coastline, the tourism industry has taken a firm hold, with Manzanillo welcoming thousands of visitors each year to its white sandy beaches and wonderful fishing. Around these beaches has sprung up many businesses to entertain and enthrall visitors to this vibrant part of Colima. Two major modern international airports, as well as over 118 miles (190 kilometers) of railways, make this a thriving area. With a total population of just under 450,000, Colima has plenty of room to grow and develop in the future.

Chiapas is a leading national producer of coffee, but it also produces rubber, *cacao*, and cattle. The state has valuable mineral resources as well, with major sources of silver, gold, and copper that remain untapped, while petroleum production has begun in earnest. The Grijalva River is also a main producer of hydroelectric power, serving the growth and expansion of industries in the area. Thirty percent of all of Mexico's hydrological resources are in Chiapas, with its three dams generating 58 percent of the hydroelectricity output and 2.2 percent of the nation's total electricity production. This makes it a vital part of the revitalization of Mexico and of the Chiapas region. With four airports and several large airfields, as well as over 8,700 miles (14,000 kilometers) of highways and railways, Chiapas is poised to become a vital trading partner not for only the United States but also for the rest of Latin America.

Due to the growth of interest in its Mayan ruins, Chiapas has begun to develop a large tourist base using the Mundo Maya travel circuit. A program designed by the Mexican government, its intention is to showcase the Mayan ruins and create the infrastructure needed to

Three women lace shoes at a shoe factory. Colima and Oaxaca are known for their production of leather goods such as shoes.

accommodate the many tourists who want to visit and admire these ancient ruins deep in the Lacandon jungle. An unfortunate side effect of this development is that with the jungle being cut back for development and the trees burnt off for cattle grazing, the original inhabitants of these areas are being forced to move away from their ancestral lands.

Guerrero's strength lies primarily in its tourist industry, with Acapulco famous worldwide for its hot and sunny beaches. With two international airports and over 4,970 miles (8,000 kilometers) of highways and roads, easy access is available to both tourists and to manufacturers.

Acapulco is only part of a major tourist development strategy in Mexico, however. Taxco, a small colonial town known for its silver; Ixtapa; and Zihuatanejo all provide most of the same tourist attractions as Acapulco, but at a slower pace.

While tourism is a major part of Guerrero's economy, other industries are beginning to come to the forefront as the overall

32

A woman picks shade-grown coffee beans on her father's farm in northern Oaxaca. Coffee is one of the major export crops of both Chiapas and Oaxaca.

Mexican economy improves and allows new expansion and innovations. Metallurgy, or working with gold and silver, has taken an important role in the revitalization of the area, as the reputation of Taxco silver rises around the world. The local resources of silver and gold mean that the talented artisans in the area already have easy access to supplies. Other industries present in the state include food and coffee processing. With the tropical climate, it is hard to grow crops, so Guerrero depends more on its natural resources rather than agriculture.

The major economic industry in Oaxaca is agriculture, with the state leading all others in coffee production. Sugarcane and tobacco

are also common crops, with cattle raising and fruit orchards plentiful in the area.

The fertile ground offers up good harvests, but it also hides a great wealth of mineral deposits, especially coal and iron. Major deposits of marble and granite can be found specifically on the isthmus, and *graphite*, *mica*, and *uranium* are scattered throughout the state. Unfortunately, many of these resources are not yet being mined, but in the future, as Mexico continues to modernize its cities and industries, these minerals will be developed as well.

Three industrial areas on Oaxaca offer processing centers for the minerals that are being mined, as well as production of such items as cement and frozen foods. Two major areas of development by the government involve the soft drink industry and the manufacturing and exporting of high-quality reproductions of pre-Columbian jewelry.

A harvest of Mexican coconuts, one of the main crops of Colima.

Oaxaca is known worldwide for the hand-woven textiles and leather goods made by the local craftsmen. The pottery created by the residents is also popular in many countries, reminders of the ancient peoples who occupied this area for centuries.

With three international airports and a large harbor situated at Salina Cruz, Oaxaca offers easy access to the rest of the world and to their markets.

In January 1994, the North American Free Trade Agreement (NAFTA) went into effect between Mexico, Canada, and the United States. The agreement eliminates restrictions on the flow of goods, services, and investments, such as tariffs (taxes imposed by the government on imported goods). It allows free trade between the countries.

NAFTA has helped the *maquiladora* industry in the states of Mexico's Pacific South. A maquiladora is a Mexican factory that is allowed to import duty-free (without tax) the materials and equipment needed to produce goods. Most maquiladoras produce electronics, textiles, and auto parts and accessories.

Until recently, these states had no big industries. Instead, most factories were small businesses where silver jewelry or local clothing was made. The governments of these states have tried to attract bigger businesses, and in 1998 large plants were built for the production of foods such as chocolate and citrus fruit products. In the same year, the first maquiladoras were also built in this region, especially in the

The evening sun silhouettes an oil platform off the coast of Mexico. Industrial work has become a major source of income for skilled laborers.

THE PACIFIC SOUTH STATES OF MEXICO

COLIMA

Per capita income: 14,621 pesos

Natural resources: iron ore

GDP in thousands of pesos:
23,551,976

Percentage of GDP:
Manufacturing 11%
Commerce 50%
Service industries 39%

Exports: lemons, corn, rice, mangos, bananas, coconuts

GUERRERO

Per capita income: 7,573 pesos

Natural resources: Beautiful beaches to attract tourists.

GDP in thousands of pesos:
73,427,393

Percentage of GDP:
Manufacturing 15%
Commerce 48%
Service industries 36%
Other 1%

Exports: silver, gold

CHIAPAS

Per capita income: 6,123 pesos

Resources: silver, gold, copper, petroleum, hydroelectric power

GDP in thousands of pesos:
69,755,324

Percentage of GDP:
Manufacturing 12%
Commerce 55%
Service industries 33%

Exports: coffee, rubber, cacao, cattle

OAXACA

Per capita income: 6,172 pesos

Resources: coal, iron, marble, granite

GDP in thousands of pesos:
64,708,914

Percentage of GDP:
Manufacturing 17%
Commerce 47%
Service industries 36%

Exports: cement, frozen foods, textiles, leather goods, fruit, jewelry, coffee, soft drinks, tobacco, sugar cane

northern part of Guerrero. In one year, these helped to increase the state's export income by 30 percent. The region is hopeful that this positive trend will continue.

Recently, maquiladoras have caused international concern because of the unsafe and unfair working conditions that exist in many of these factories. Maquiladoras do help bring foreign investment to the states of the Pacific South however.

PER CAPITA INCOME = the amount earned in an area divided by the total number of people living in that area
GDP = Gross Domestic Product, the total value of goods and services produced during the year
1 PESO = about $0.11, as of January 2002

Figures from INEGI, the Mexican National Institute of Statistics, based on Mexico's 2000 census.

This terracotta dog sculpture found in Colima was created approximately 1,500 years ago.

THE CULTURE

Colima, like many Mexican states, shares many holidays with other parts of the country. But some *fiestas* are specifically for certain churches or communities, and each year both the people of the region and tourists enjoy the celebration. Here is a list of the most popular festivals in the capital city of Colima.

* **Fiesta de la Virgen de la Salud**
January 23–February 2.
Centered in the northern part of town around Gallardo and Corregidora Avenues. Here you can find crafts, food, wonderful folk dancing and fireworks to go along with the parade.

* **Fiesta Charrotaurina**
February 7–23
In Villa de Alvarez, a few miles northwest of Colima City. Processions start from the Jardín de Libertad; leading to carnivals and festive displays; you might even see a bullfight as well.

✳ Fiesta de San José
March 9–19.
Centered on the west side near Quintero and Suárez, religious processions are common in this festival, along with a variety of local crafts and dancing for the tourist.

The Casa de Cultura of Colima also sponsors an annual fine arts festival in late November and early December. Everything from ballet to opera to painting will be on exhibit, displaying the best the area has to offer.

And if you visit Colima, be sure to pick up one of the most popular tourist items, a replica of the famous Colima Dog. Statues like this have been found throughout the area at various archeological sites. They have been reproduced many times over for the eager tourist looking for a novel souvenir.

A majority of the inhabitants of Chiapas are the descendants of the original Mayan tribes who lived there. For centuries, they have resisted outside control and demanded their part of the riches being reaped from the soil. As a result, constant turmoil between the local rebels and the Mexican government sometimes leads to armed conflict. When the average pay consists of only nine U.S. dollars a day, it's not hard to imagine the frustration and anger of the residents who look to the north and see the riches of the United States. Immigration is a major industry here as well, with many men leaving their families to try and work legally or illegally across the border. They do not believe the Mexican government's assurances that the economy will improve quickly so that they will not have to seek their fortunes elsewhere. As a result, many villages have very few

Zapatista rebels take a break in the La Candona jungle near Chiapas in January 1994. The goal of the Zapatista Army for National Liberation is independence from Mexico for the state of Chiapas.

men of working age, with a majority of the males being either too young to leave or retired workers living on a meager (or nonexistent) *pension*.

The rebels are called the Zapatista Army for National Liberation, and their goal is the eventual independence of Chiapas. With the new government elected in 2000; the rebels are finally being given a voice and progress is being made in the areas of Indian rights and local control over resources.

Despite their poverty and rebellion, the people of Chiapas still love to celebrate. Some of their major holidays include:

✳ **Chiapas de Corzo's San Sebastián Festival**
January 15–23

✳ **Carnival and Easter Week in San Juan Charmula**
Held every Friday during Lent, this festival includes the local villagers walking over hot coals!

✳ **Chamula's San Juan Festival**
June 22–24

Townsfolk costumed as skeletons carry a coffin through the streets in a mock funeral during the Day of the Dead, which celebrates the souls of friends and family members who have passed away. Day of the Dead celebrations may appear strange to outsiders, but they carry a great deal of significance for Mexican participants.

✳ Festival of the Patron Saint of San Christóbal
July 24–25
During this time brightly decorated trucks, buses, and cars parade up a hilltop to the San Christóbal Church for the celebration and ceremonies of this religious holiday.

✳ Celebration of San Lorenzo in Zinacantan
August 6–11

✳ Día de los Muertos (The Day of the Dead)
October 31–November 2
Celebrated throughout Mexico, this event includes festive grave-side celebrations and enchanting colorful costumes.

The Virgin Mary holds special religious meaning to devout Christian Mexicans. She is often called Our Lady of Guadalupe, because she appeared to a Mexican man in Guadalupe in 1531. During parades in her honor, the image of Mary is carried through the streets to the church built where she is believed to have appeared.

* **The Feast of the Virgin of Guadalupe**
  December 12 (although in Tuxtla Gutiérrez, it's celebrated for an entire week!)

* **Día de la Mexicanidad**
  September 14
  Celebrated in every village and city in Chiapas, this holiday commemorates the independence of Chiapas from Guatemala and its entrance into Mexico as a state.

Many residents of Guerrero are descendants of the Olmecs, though their ancestors also came from a variety of other civilizations, including the Spanish. Today, many of these people make their living working in or around the hotels and the beaches. There the beautiful and creative arts and crafts of the Guerrero citizens can be seen and bought by any visitor. Many craft markets feature brightly colored masks and almost garishly painted wooden fish and ceramics, all reflecting the ancient culture of their makers.

Mexican actors play the roles of Jesus and a Roman soldier during a Holy Week festival. This reenacting of the crucifixion is one of the most symbolic and emotional rituals of the year for Christian Mexicans.

Like all the other Mexican states, the people of Guerrero love to celebrate. Here are some of their festivals:

* **The Feast of Santa Prisca and San Sebastián**
January 18–20
Held in Taxco, this celebration is for the town's patron saints with plenty of fireworks and music and parties.

* **Holy Week** (from Palm Sunday to Easter Sunday)

Much like the rest of Mexico, Guerrero holds this major Catholic event in high esteem; merging Christian and Indian traditions within the ceremonies. Images have a more Indian look to them as the local inhabitants use the ritual and the ceremony as a personal mirror to reflect their community.

* **Día de San Miguel** (Saint Michael's Day)
September 29
Dances and pilgrimages to churches celebrate this religious holiday.

✳ The Fiesta de los Jumil

November 1–2

Following the Day of the Dead celebrations (throughout Mexico), the Taxco people will head for a nearby hill outside the city. Here they will capture the *jumil*, crawling insects somewhat like ants or beetles, and eat them, either alive or cooked in a stew or a fried dish, usually with plenty of hot sauce. The jumil is said to taste like iodine but is considered a great treat by the local people who eagerly anticipate this holiday.

✳ Jornadas Alarconianos

The biggest celebration in Taxco, this festival honors one of Mexico's most famous writers with theater, dance and concerts rotating around this famous writer. Juan Ruiz de Alarcon y Mendoza was born in 1581 and died in 1639, but he is still famous for his plays and comedies. Born in Mexico, he studied law in Spain and became a member of the governing body for the Spanish colonies (including Mexico at the time) in 1626. The actual dates for this celebration vary each year, but the fiestas include Taxco's famous fireworks as well as music and dancing into the early hours of the morning. Popular with tourists and local inhabitants alike, this festival is a major yearly event.

In Oaxaca, a majority of the people are almost direct descendants of the native Zapotec and Miztec, who built such archeological wonders as Mitla and Monte Albán. The state's culture reflects these ancient civilizations. Brightly woven textiles and skillfully created jewelry and pottery attest to the influences of these long-ago people.

46

Two out of three Oxaquernos (inhabitants of Oaxaca) can trace their lineage back to the Zapotec and Miztec cultures. However, they speak 16 different languages and over 50 individual dialects. To many of these people, Spanish is a second language if it is learned at all. Oaxaca has one of the highest native populations in all of Mexico.

Due to the influence of the Spanish invaders, the majority of the people are Roman Catholic, with very few Protestants. The church and monastery of Santo Domingo, located in Oaxaca City itself, is a national monument drawing tourists and local worshippers alike to the classical architecture. As with many other states in Mexico, some holidays combine the feast days of Catholic saints with native religious elements.

✳ The Day of the Dead
October 31–November 2
As in the rest of the country, Oaxauernos celebrate this holiday by visiting graveyards and holding celebrations. These often involve whole families having picnics in the cemeteries with the favorite food of the deceased. Many villages have large parties; the most popular of these is in Xoxo, but the celebrations in Atzompa and Xochimilco are well known as well. The festivals and parties are open to everyone, and tourists are welcome.

✳ Noche de Rábanos (Night of the Radishes)
December 23
For this celebration the local market is transformed into a wonderful art display as local growers and artists display their radish crops

and creations. Ranging from Nativity displays to the Space Shuttle, the artistic competition is judged not only on the complexity but also on the size and quality of the radishes. Other creations involve dried flowers and cornhusks.

✳ **Guelaguetza** (Zapotec for "offering" or "gift")
Held the last two Mondays each July, this is a major state celebration that takes place in Oaxaca City. Dancers from all the cities and villages meet in Oaxaca City, bringing the best their area has to offer, from coffee to fruit and everything in between. Meeting at the Guelaguetza Auditorium; dancers perform complicated and elaborate dances for an entire day in the open spaces of the auditorium. Wearing authentic costumes handed down throughout the years, they recreate the feeling of their ancestors who also celebrated the wealth of their territory.

Throughout the Pacific South, celebrations brighten the lives of the people who live there. These colorful fiestas attract tourists to the wonderful culture of this area.

	STATE POPULATION	GROWTH RATE
Chiapas	3,920,892	2.0%
Colima	542,627	2.4%
Guerrero	3,079,649	1.6%
Oaxaca	3,438,765	1.3%

Mexico's ethnic groups
Indian-Spanish (mestizo): 60%
Indian: 30%
White: 9%
Other: 1%

Education 12 years of education is required from ages 6 through 18. About 94% of school-age children are enrolled in school. The literacy rate is 89%.

Mexico's religions
Roman Catholic: 89%
Protestant: 6%
Other: 5%

This relief sculpture in Michoacan shows the conquistador Gonzalo de Sandoval receiving a gift from the king of Colima in 1521.

THE CITIES AND COMMUNITIES

Colima's capital city is also called Colima. Almost exactly in the center of the triangle-shaped state, it is also known as "The City of the Palm Trees" due to the wonderful vegetation around and inside the city. With approximately 160,000 inhabitants, Colima has many wonderful tourist attractions, from the Zócalo (Main Square) with its beautiful trees and architecture, to the Cathedral (finished in 1824), to the many museums displaying ancient art, musical instruments, and ceremonial masks.

Walking into Colima's center you'll find a variety of places to visit: from the Jardin de Libertad (Garden of Liberty) where you can find stores carrying anything and everything, to the Museo de Historia (Museum of History) where you can view wonderfully preserved pre-Columbian pottery. Connected by highway to Guadalajara, this capital city boasts a wonderful variety of Mexican foods, as well as a large and recognized university.

50

Perched on the Pacific Coast is Manzanillo, the main port of Colima. In 1522, Gonzalo de Sandoval dropped anchor just north of Manzanillo Bay in the Bay of Salagua. He was searching for safe sites for travelers to land and venture ashore, but he moved onward into the center of Colima, leaving the bay behind. It wasn't until 1527 that Manzanillo Bay was fully explored by navigator Alvaro de Saavedra. First named Santiago's Bay of Good Hope, it soon became a popular site for expeditions both arriving and leaving through the not-so-safe waters. Pirates swept up and down the Pacific Coast at this time, seeking treasure and finding it in the *galleons* that left Santiago's Bay loaded with gold, silver, and copper.

In 1825, the port of Manzanillo, named after the numerous groves of *manzanillo* trees that flourished on the shore, was officially opened. Over the years the importance of the seaport grew. In 1915, it was declared the state capital when Pancho Villa's troops threatened to capture the city of Colima.

Thanks to a major renovation a few years ago, the harbor has become accessible to all major shipping lines and their vessels. This has helped the city to grow even more, and brought more visitors. Tourists can fish or take advantage of the many wonderful beaches that line the coast. Manzanillo also boasts many other attractions, among them a *mural* done by local artist Jorge Chavez Carrillo and the University Museum of Archaeology in San Pedrito.

Further down the coast from Manzarillo is Tecomán, one of the most popular coastal towns. Famous for its seafood, the restaurants here offer more than the usual choices. On the menu you can find shellfish soup and

A bird's-eye view of Manzanillo, the main port of Colima and one of the state's most important cities.

octopus. A nearby favorite fishing spot is the Amelo Lagoon, located just one hour from Tecomán on the main highway. Here the avid fisherman can enjoy one of the best fishing experiences possible anywhere.

Coquimatlán lies just west of Colima and offers the visitor an old-fashioned atmosphere with cobbled streets far from the hustle and bustle of the big city. Each year this city is witness to the most traditional religious celebration in the entire state—the carrying of the "Señor de la Expiración" (Lord of the Expiration) from the Church of San Pedro inside Coquimatlán to the nearby town of Rancho de Villa. Held on the first Tuesday of every January, many street dances and fairs are held here.

And if you want to get a closer look at volcanoes, there is no better place than the Nevado de Colima National Park, right at the

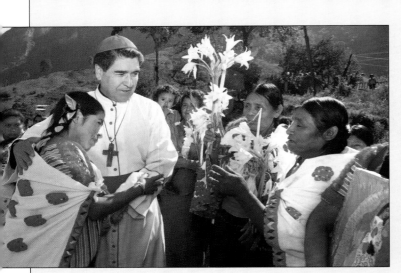

The bishop of San Cristóbal de las Casas, in Chiapas, is greeted by Tzotzil Indians and mestizos before a procession to San Pedro Church in Arizmendi.

northeast edge of the state. Ideal for mountaineering and camping, you may also have the opportunity to venture close to Volcan de Fuego, an active volcano.

San Cristóbal de las Casas is still one of Chiapas' main cities, although no longer the capital. Near the center of the state, this ancient city offers many attractions to the average tourist, not least of which is the charming atmosphere. Tourists feel as though they travel back in time at the many craft shops and stores. With a population of approximately 150,000, the city sits at an altitude of 6,888 feet (2,100 meters) above sea level and offers a central hub for tourists traveling to the archeological sites nearby.

In 1892, Tuxtla Gutiérrez replaced San Cristóbal as the capital city of Chiapas. With a thriving population of 390,000, this city is rapidly transforming its historical buildings and ancient homes to a thriving metropolitan center as it moves forward into the 21st century. It is home to one of the most innovative zoos in the world, the Miguel Alvarez del Toro Zoo (also known as ZooMAT). Here all the animals are native to Chiapas and Mexico, and all run free in their natural habitat for visitors to watch and admire. Botanical gardens and museums also help make Tuxtla Gutiérrez a worthwhile destination for any tourist. Not too far from the city are the Mayan ruins of Bonampak and Yaxchilán, offering visitors a wonderful archeological experience.

Acapulco is one of the best known cites of Guerrero, if not Mexico itself. Originally used as a major port for the Spanish to ferry their treasures from their conquests around the world, this city has become world renowned for its beaches and tourist industry.

Taxco is one of the smaller but still popular cities, situated at the foothills of the Sierra Madre. Famous for their silverware, the skilled

The beaches of southwestern Mexico are a great draw for tourists. One of the most popular destinations is Acapulco, Guerrero, where luxury hotels overlook the white sands and clear waters.

artisans of this city are descended from the original immigrants who came here centuries ago to search for silver. After the original silver rush in the 1500s, interest tapered off in this area due to low silver levels—until the 1700s, when a Frenchman discovered a thick rich vein that revitalized the silver industry and boosted the local economy once again. But it was an American, William G. Spratling from New Orleans, who really set Taxco's wheels in motion. Falling quickly in love with Taxco, he set up a shop and began to produce silver jewelry based on pre-Columbian designs and artwork. He drew in local townsfolk as his *apprentices*, and soon his work earned Taxco worldwide recognition and fame. Many of his descendants and their apprentices carry on this rich tradition to this day.

Chilpancingo, the capital city of Guerrero, is approximately 80 miles (130 kilometers) from Acapulco near the center of the state. With a population of 97,000, this city is also known as Chilpancingo de los Bravos. The extended name honors its local heroes in the war against Spain, three brothers, the most famous of whom was Nicholas Bravo. The city serves as the regional center for the agricultural products grown in the area

Like Acapulco, Ixtapa and Zihuatanejo attract tourists, but they are much less built up and modernized. Offering a quieter, gentler atmosphere, these two towns have sports fishing and an abundance of restaurants and hotels. They cater to the visitor who is looking for a relaxing visit to Mexico.

Oaxaca City, in the state of Oaxaca, lies in a valley surrounded by low mountains, near the center of the state. Its full name is Oaxaca de Juárez, in honor of President Benito Juárez. According to Aztec folklore, the city's original name was Huasyacac, and it was founded in 1486, during the time that the Aztecs ruled over the Miztecs and Zapotecs. Active in the Mexican Revolution against Spain and later in the resistance against the French, this city is famous for its hand-wrought gold and silver as well as its artisans' handicrafts and artwork. Unfortunately, the city has suffered damage from ongoing earthquakes.

Monte Albán, a short daytrip away from Oaxaca, is one of the state's treasures. Overlooking the Oaxaca Valley at 1,300 feet (396 meters), this city is well over a thousand years old and provides glimpses of the Zapotec culture.

Mitla lies just southeast of Oaxaca, and its history is much like Monte Albán's. But what makes this city interesting for scholars are the strange geometric patterns found everywhere. The designs contain not a single image of a person nor any depiction of events; they are nothing but abstract designs carved into brilliant stones. The name comes from the Aztec word "mictlán" or "place of the dead."

Taxco, located in the Sierra Madres, is an important city in Guerrero.

CHRONOLOGY

3000 B.C.	Olmecs live in what is now Guerrero.
200 B.C.–A.D. 900	The Maya settle in Oaxaca and Chiapas.
1200s	Monte Albán becomes part of the Miztec culture; Mitla as well is settled and the vast murals are produced making it unlike any other city in the world.
1420–1500	Aztecs take over the center of the Mexican Valley and begin to expand their empire. Eventually they rule most of Mexico, dominating the culture and the other native people still present.
1517	The Spanish arrive in Mexico. Chiapas becomes a part of Guatemala under the Conquistadors.
1523	Colima City founded.
1810–1821	Mexican War of Independence is fought against Spain.
1824	Chiapas gains independence from Guatemala and joins Mexico as a free state.
1829	President Vicente Guerrero abolishes slavery in Mexico; years before the United States.
1849	State of Guerrero created from land taken from other nearby states.
1858	Benito Juárez, originally from Oaxaca, becomes president of Mexico.
1877	Porfirio Díaz, also of Oaxaca, takes control of the government.

1880 Railroad built across Colima from Capital City to Manzanillo by Porfirio Díaz, enabling transportation of materials both into and out of the interior.

1892 The capital of Chiapas moved from San Cristóbal to Tuxtla Gutiérrez.

1910–1917 Major damage done to the Colima area in the Mexican Revolution.

1974 Discovery of major crude petroleum deposits in Chiapas with further exploration and development following.

1993 President Carlos Salinas de Gortari signs the North American Free Trade Agreement (NAFTA) with United States President George Bush.

1994 Violence breaks out in Chiapas from Zapista rebels who want independence.

2000 Vicente Fox, originally from Chiapas, is elected president.

2001 Promising reforms, Fox's government holds discussions with the Zapistas as well as other rebel factions.

2002 Latin American leaders, including Mexico's Vicente Fox, meet in Argentina for the Global Alumni Conference to discuss technological and economic issues.

FOR MORE INFORMATION

CHIAPAS

Government of Chiapas
www.chiapas.gob.mx

State Tourism Office
Blvd. Belisario Dominguez No. 950
Planta Baja
CP 29060 Tuxtla Gutiérrez, Chis.
Tel: (961) 3-9396
Fax: (961) 2-5509

COLIMA

Government of Colima
www.colima.gob.mx

State Tourism Office
Portal Hidalgo No. 96 Centro
CP 28000 Colima, Col.
Tel: (331) 2-4360
Fax: (331) 2-8360
E-mail: turisco@palmera.
    colimanet.com

GUERRERO

Government of Guerrero
www.guerrero.gob.mx

State Tourism Office
Av. Costera Miguel Alemán No. 4455
Centro Cultural y de Convenciones
de Acapulco
Fracc. Club Deportivo
CP 39850 Acapulco, Gro.
Tel: (74) 84-2423
Fax: (74) 81-1160

OAXACA

Government of Oaxaca
www.oaxaca.gob.mx

State Tourism Office
Independencia No. 607 esq.
García Vigil
CP 68000 Oaxaca, Oax.
Tel: (951) 6-0717
Fax: (951) 6-1500
E-mail: info@oaxaca-travel.gob.mx

THINGS TO DO AND SEE

COLIMA

Fuego de Colima and Volcán de Fuego, and active volcano

Fishing in Manzanillo

CHIAPAS

San Cristóbal's historical sites

Huixtan and Oxchuc, two small villages known for the exquisite colors of their embroidery

Palengque, an ancient Mayan site

GUERRERO

The Cacahuamilpa caverns

The cliff divers of La Quebrada in Acapulco

The underwater shrine just south of the Pensisula de las Playas, a submerged bronze statue of the Virgin of Guadalupe

OAXACA

The popular archeological sites and museum at Monte Albán

The resort at Huatulco, a government project to encourage tourism

Resort attractions at Puerto Escondido

GLOSSARY

Apprentices	Students who train under an expert.
Asset	Resource or benefit.
Cacao	The bean used to make chocolate.
Conquistadors	Spanish conquerors of the New World.
Dyewoods	Wood used for making dyes.
Fiestas	Spanish parties or celebrations.
Galleons	Heavy, square-rigged sailing ships used in the 15th to the early 18th centuries, especially by the Spanish.
Graphite	A soft black form of carbon used to make lead pencils, electrolytic anodes, and nuclear reactors.
Infrastructure	A country's public works, such as roads, railroads, and schools.
Mahogany	A reddish-brown hard wood from a tropical tree.
Malaria	A disease caused by one-celled parasites; spread to humans by mosquitoes.
Manzanillo	A small apple.
Mica	A mineral that can be separated into very thin, transparent layers.
Mural	A large picture painted on a wall.
Pension	Money paid by the government or a business to a person after retirement.
Plateau	High, flat land.
Rosewood	The reddish wood from a tropical tree.
Smallpox	A contagious disease that causes high fevers and pus-filled sores that leave deep scars.
Uranium	A heavy, silvery, radioactive element.

FURTHER READING

Burke, Michael E. *Hippocrene Companion Guide to Mexico*. New York: Hippocrene Books, 1992.

Coe, Michael D. Coe. *Mexico*. New York: Thames and Hudson, 1994.

Collis, John and David M. Jones, editors. *Blue Guide Mexico*. New York: Norton, 1997.

Fodor's Mexico 2001. New York: Fodor's Travel Publications, 2001.

Let's Go: Mexico. New York: Let's Go, Inc., 2001.

Mexico Travel Book. Tampa, Fla.: AAA Publishing, 2000.

Wilcock, John, Kal Muller, and Martha Ellen Zenfell, editors. *Insight Guides, Mexico*. New York: Langenscheidt Publishers, 1998.

INTERNET RESOURCES

INEGI (Geographic, Demographic, and Economic Information of Mexico)
http://www.inegi.gob.mx/diffusion/ingles/portadai.html

Mesoweb
http://www.mesoweb.com/welcome.html#externalresources

Mexico for Kids
http://www.elbalero.gob.mx/index_kids.html

Mexico Channel
http://www.mexicochannel.net

INDEX

PICTURE CREDITS

2:      © OTTN Publsing
3:      Corbis Images
10:     Corbis Images
13:     Danny Lehman/Corbis
14:     Charles and Josette Lenars/Corbis
15:     Roger Ressmeyer/Corbis
16:     Daniel Lain/Corbis
20:     Corbis Images
23:     Historical Picture Archive/Corbis
24:     Daniel Aguilar/Reuters
25:     Corbis Images
26:     Werner Forman/Art Resource
28:     Dave G. Houser/Houserstock
31:     Danny Lehman/Corbis
32:     Liaison/Newsmakers/Online USA

33:     Nik Wheeler/Corbis
34:     Credit: Larry Lee Photography/Corbis
38:     North Carolina Museum of Art/Corbis
41:     Liaison/Newsmakers/Online USA
42:     Reuters NewMedia Inc./Corbis
43:     Fulvio Roiter/Corbis
44:     Hulton/Archive
48:     Charles and Josette Lenars/Corbis
51:     Corbis Images
52:     AFP/Corbis
53:     Corbis Images
55:     Corbis Images

Cover   (front) Corbis Images
        (inset) IMS Communications, Ltd.
        (back) Corbis Images

CONTRIBUTORS

Roger E. Hernández is the most widely syndicated columnist writing on Hispanic issues in the United States. His weekly column, distributed by King Features, appears in some 40 newspapers across the country, including the *Washington Post*, *Los Angeles Daily News*, *Dallas Morning News*, *Arizona Republic*, *Rocky Mountain News* in Denver, *El Paso Times*, and *Hartford Courant*. He is also the author of *Cubans in America*, an illustrated history of the Cuban presence in what is now the United States, from the early colonists in 16th-century Florida to today's Castro-era exiles. The book was designed to accompany a PBS documentary of the same title.

Hernández's articles and essays have been published in the *New York Times*, *New Jersey Monthly*, *Reader's Digest*, and *Vista Magazine*; he is a frequent guest on television and radio political talk shows, and often travels the country to lecture on his topic of expertise. Currently, he is teaching journalism and English composition at the New Jersey Institute of Technology in Newark, where he holds the position of writer-in-residence. He is also a member of the adjunct faculty at Rutgers University.

Hernández left Cuba with his parents at the age of nine. After living in Spain for a year, the family settled in Union City, New Jersey, where Hernandez grew up. He attended Rutgers University, where he earned a BA in Journalism in 1977; after graduation, he worked in television news before moving to print journalism in 1983. He lives with his wife and two children in Upper Montclair, New Jersey.

Randi Field is a freelance writer, editor, and lawyer in Silver Spring, Maryland. She has written numerous articles on law, science, and education for the American Bar Association's *Mental & Physical Disability Law Reporter*, the Smithsonian Institute's National Academy of Sciences, MedLearn, and WebMD. She practiced law for 11 years in Washington, D.C., in private practice and for the U.S. International Trade Commission and the Washington Legal Clinic for the Homeless. She has two children, Jared and Casey McGrath, both students at St. Bernadette School in Silver Spring.